MW01154812

THIS IS A BOOK ABOUT NOODLES

BRENDAN PANG

Author of
This is a Book About Dumplings

First published in 2022 by

Page Street Publishing Co.

27 Congress Street, Suite 1511

Salem, MA 01970

www.pagestreetpublishing.com

Distributed by Macmillan, sales in Canada by The Canadian Manda Group.

26 25 24 23 22 1 2 3 4 5

ISBN-13: 978-1-64567-578-5

ISBN-10: 1-64567-578-5

Library of Congress Control Number: 2021951126

Cover and book design by Kylie Alexander for Page Street Publishing Co.

Photography by Thomas Davidson

Printed and bound in China

Page Street Publishing protects our planet by donating to nonprofits like The Trustees, which focuses on local land conservation.

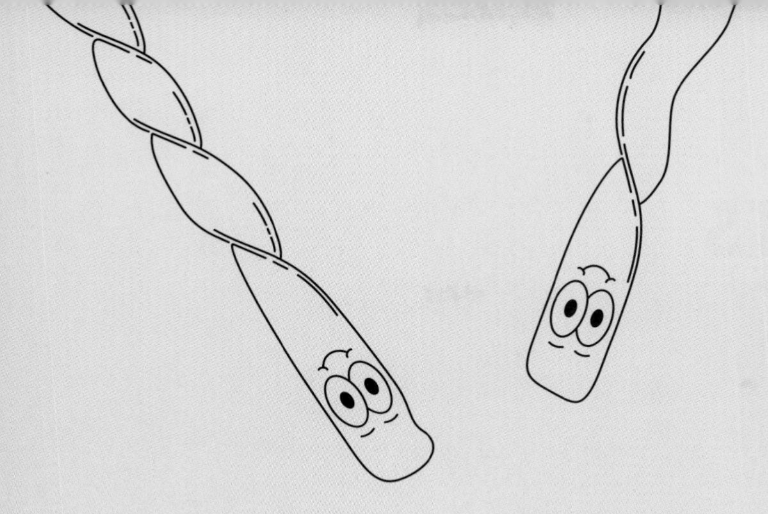

I WOULD LIKE TO ACKNOWLEDGE THE WHADJUK NOONGAR PEOPLE—PAST, PRESENT AND EMERGING—FOR THIS BOOK. THE IDEAS, RECIPES AND FOOD WITHIN WERE CREATED ON THEIR LANDS AND USING THE PRODUCE FROM IT.

THIS BOOK WAS WRITTEN IN LOVING MEMORY OF MY GRANDPÈRE, CLEMENT KON-YU. FROM THE TIME I WAS ABLE TO WALK, HE TAUGHT ME HOW TO EAT WELL, AND TO SHARE MY FOOD WITH THOSE AROUND ME. THIS BOOK WOULD NOT BE POSSIBLE WITHOUT HIS LOVE AND SUPPORT.

CONTENTS

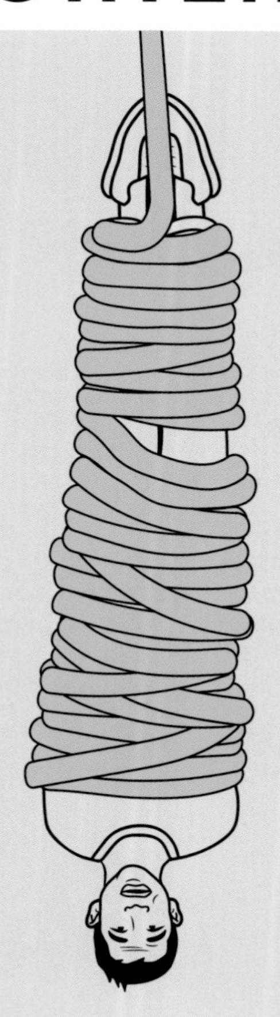

INTRODUCTION

One of my earliest memories, and certainly one of my fondest, is making fresh noodles with Grandmère and Grandpère. As for so many families, across the globe and in a multitude of cultures, noodles represent so much more than just food to me.

Growing up, we had noodles in every style I could imagine (and even some I couldn't!) for all sorts of occasions and purposes. I didn't just grow up with noodles, I grew up *on* noodles.

So, I've always been fascinated with noodles—their long and intriguing history, their deep and enduring cultural heritage and, in particular, their exceptional versatility.

Noodles don't belong to just one cuisine, or one type of dish, or one form or a method of application. There are extra-long noodles, short noodles, fat noodles, thin noodles, curly noodles, crunchy noodles, soft noodles, transparent noodles . . . noodles of every color and noodles made from a myriad of ingredients. There are simple, plain noodle dishes and there are rich, complex ones. You can have noodles fried, boiled, crispy, in soup, in gravy . . . they can take center stage or just be the humble sidekick. There are countless noodle dishes, and oodles more are created every day in restaurants, homes, street vendor carts, in any kind of kitchen around the world.

And that's the inspiration behind this book. Just like my first book about dumplings, it's a simple declaration that everyone can cook, and cook well! These noodle recipes can easily be cooked at home and are best made fresh; however, if short on time, store-bought noodles will also do the trick!

One of the main reasons I love to cook is that it allows me to create, which lets me (and anyone!) explore and express that creativity. And to a chef, noodles may just be the perfect tool.

This book represents just a small selection of the many noodle dishes I've had the pleasure of tasting, and also features my own interpretations of some more popular dishes. It's almost an impossible task trying to curate a recipe book with the hundreds of options available, and this certainly isn't a comprehensive list, but it offers a "degustation" of some of my favorites.

Thank you for reading this book! As you explore the world of noodles—*your* world of noodles—I hope that I don't just provide a guide to your cooking, but also spark some creativity of your own. I look forward to one day tasting some of the marvelous creations that these recipes may inspire.

ONE

WHEAT NOODLES

Why wheat? Well, wheat is the OG, baby! After millet was (literally) left in the dust, the Han Dynasty (AD 25–220) recorded one of the earliest historical noodle recipes in China, which involved ripping up a breadlike cake and boiling these pieces in a hot broth, called *mian pian*.

After the millet-based and mian pian noodles, the increasing use of wheat in subsequent Chinese dynasties truly opened the art and tradition of noodle making, through the characteristic "stretch" that gluten brings, and along with it, noodles in all shapes, sizes and lengths. Today, wheat-based noodles are one of the most widely used and renowned—throughout China and all over the world—and for most people, our first noodle is a wheat-based one!

Not everyone has made noodles from scratch before, but it's likely that most of us have played with a bit of dough! A little stint in the kitchen with any wheat-based bread or pastry is a great foundation to start from, especially if you've never worked with a dough before.

This chapter contains some traditional methods that will introduce you to working a wheat-based dough from scratch, using different techniques to create different shapes and sizes. Best of all—no equipment is required!

The Lanzhou Beef Hand-Pulled Noodles (page 12), Hand-Smacked Hot Sauce Noodles (page 15) and Hot Udon Noodles (page 19) are some of the noodles that woke me to the way of wheat.

In later chapters, we'll also explore some unconventional and wonderful styles of noodles with non-run-of-the-mill ingredients, but wheat flour is definitely the cornerstone of noodle-making and is widely accessible and relatively inexpensive.

BEIJING FRIED SAUCE NOODLES

Mom Dumpling House (one of my favorite Chinese restaurants in Perth, Australia) introduced me to *zha jiang mian* (Beijing fried sauce noodles). This simple and very popular dish is considered to be one of the most traditional dishes in China but features just four main elements—noodles (of course), pork, vegetables and a special bean-based sauce. One of the main characteristics of *lao Beijing cai* ("Old Beijing food") is saltiness. The noodles in this dish provide the perfect instrument for the salty soybean-based sauce to cling to, with some fresh vegetables to lighten the flavor. It's also an easy one to make vegan with the omission of the ground pork. This a great starter recipe if you haven't made noodles before, especially as hand-cut noodles don't have to, and shouldn't, be perfect—but they'll still be delicious. Simple, fresh, tasty.

SERVES 4

Marinated Pork

6 oz (170 g) fatty ground pork

Pinch of salt

1 tsp cornstarch

1 tsp vegetable oil

Pinch of freshly ground white pepper

Noodle Sauce

1 tbsp (15 ml) vegetable oil

1 tbsp (5 g) minced fresh ginger

1 tbsp (10 g) minced garlic

6 fresh shiitake mushrooms, finely chopped

2 tbsp (30 ml) sweet bean sauce (see notes)

3 tbsp (45 ml) ground bean sauce (see notes)

1 tbsp (15 ml) dark soy sauce

1 cup + 2 tsp (250 ml) water

1 lb (450 g) ribbon-cut Hand-Cut Wheat Noodles (page 155)

1 cup (100 g) julienned cucumber

1 cup (116 g) julienned watermelon radish (see notes)

½ cup (50 g) julienned spring onion

Marinate the pork: In a medium-sized bowl, combine the pork, salt, cornstarch, vegetable oil and white pepper, and mix well. Set aside to marinate for at least 30 minutes.

When ready to cook, make the noodle sauce: Heat the vegetable oil in a wok over medium heat and add the marinated pork. Cook until browned, stirring, for 2 to 3 minutes. Add the ginger, garlic and mushrooms, and cook for another 2 to 3 minutes before adding the sweet bean sauce, ground bean sauce, dark soy sauce and water. Mix well, lower the heat and cover the wok. Simmer for 15 minutes to allow the flavors to combine and the sauce to cook through, stirring occasionally to prevent sticking.

Bring a large pot of water to a boil, then cook the noodles for about 3 minutes. Divide the noodles among four serving bowls and top with the sauce, cucumber, radish and spring onion.

NOTES:

- Sweet bean sauce is a sweetened soybean sauce. It can be found at most Asian grocers.
- Ground bean sauce is made with yellow beans and should not be confused with regular bean/soybean paste. It can be found at most Asian grocers.
- Watermelon radish can be replaced with regular radish or carrot.

LANZHOU BEEF HAND-PULLED NOODLES

Noodle-soup combo! Traditional Lanzhou (pronounced "laan-joh") beef noodles have a potent broth made using aged beef, which concentrates the meaty flavor throughout the broth. Beef is a hero of the Gansu province—where this recipe calls home—and so is the amazing art of hand-pulling noodles: where a single piece of dough is stretched repeatedly into one incredible unbroken strand!

I don't have access to aged beef, and don't have the patience to age beef myself, so my recipe uses standard beef you can get at any supermarket without compromising on the heartiness. Whereas the *zha jiang mai* noodles are simpler, the flavor of this broth is rich, well spiced and has a nice lashing of chili oil on the top for a real kick.

SERVES 6

Beef Broth

3⅓ lb (1.5 kg) beef bones

10 cups (2.4 L) water

3⅓ lb (1.5 kg) beef chuck, cut into chunks

Spices

1 cinnamon stick

2 bay leaves

5 star anise

8 cloves

2 tsp (3 g) Sichuan peppercorns

1 tsp white peppercorns

1 tsp fennel seeds

1 tsp cumin seeds

4 slices licorice root (optional)

17.5 oz (500 g) daikon radish, peeled and cut into slices

Salt

1½ lb (675 g) thin-cut Hand-Cut Wheat Noodles (page 155)

Chopped fresh cilantro, for garnish

Chopped spring onion, for garnish

Chinese Chili Oil (page 147), for serving (optional)

Preheat the oven to 400°F (200°C). Rinse the beef bones thoroughly and pat dry. Place on a baking sheet lined with parchment paper and roast in the oven for 45 minutes. Fill a large pot with the water and add the beef chuck and roasted bones. Bring to a boil over high heat, then lower the heat to low. Skim the surface and continue to do so, discarding any foam and impurities that float to the top, until the broth is clean.

Using cheesecloth and kitchen twine, tie up the spices in a bag (see note) and add to your broth. Let simmer over low heat for 2 to 3 hours, or until the beef is cooked through and tender. Add the daikon to the pot in the last 20 minutes and cook until tender. Taste and add salt until seasoned to your liking.

Bring a separate large pot of water to a boil, then cook the noodles for about 3 minutes. Drain and divide the noodles among six serving bowls and pour in the hot broth. Top with pieces of daikon and beef, and garnish with cilantro and spring onion. Finish with a generous amount of chili oil if you like it spicy!

NOTE:

- A ball-shaped tea strainer would work well to hold spices together if you do not have cheesecloth and twine.

HAND-SMACKED HOT SAUCE NOODLES

Similar in style to the hand-pulled noodles, these flat noodles are hand-smacked into shape by taking your dough and slapping it up and down on your kitchen counter as you stretch it out at either end (a bit like a skipping rope). *Biang* refers to the shape of these noodles, being thick, flat and wide like a belt, but is a bit of a double entendre, as I think it makes a "biang biang biang" sound as it stretches and slaps on the counter.

The traditional way to have this dish is *you po* (pronounced "yoh-po") style. It involves mounting all your seasonings onto your noodles and pouring some hot oil on top. I prefer to make the chili oil in advance, for all the spices to infuse. The tomato sauce might seem weird, but helps balance out the bold flavors and gives the dish a nice mouthfeel.

SERVES 4

Spiced Vinegar Sauce

¾ cup + 2 tsp (200 ml) light soy sauce

⅓ cup + 2 tsp (100 ml) Chinese black vinegar

3 tbsp + 1 tsp (50 ml) water

1 tbsp (13 g) superfine sugar

1 small cinnamon stick

1 star anise

1 bay leaf

Pinch of fennel seeds

Pinch of Sichuan peppercorns

Tomato Sauce

1 tbsp (15 ml) vegetable oil

1 (14-oz [400-g]) can whole tomatoes

3 tbsp (48 g) tomato paste

1 lb (450 g) Hand-Smacked Noodles (page 156)

Dash of sesame oil

Chinese Chili Oil (page 147)

1 cup (100 g) julienned cucumber, for garnish

½ cup (50 g) finely sliced spring onion, for garnish

Make the spiced vinegar sauce: In a small saucepan, combine all the ingredients for this sauce and simmer over low heat until fragrant, about 10 minutes. Drain through a sieve into a bowl, discard the spices and set the sauce aside.

Make the tomato sauce: In a blender, combine all the ingredients for this sauce and blitz on high speed. Transfer to a small pot and cook over medium heat, stirring, until thickened, 6 to 8 minutes. Set aside.

Bring a large pot of water to a boil, then cook the noodles for 3 to 4 minutes. Drain and transfer to a bowl. Toss with a dash of sesame oil to stop them from sticking.

Divide your noodles among four serving bowls. Add a generous amount of the tomato sauce, spiced vinegar sauce and Chinese Chili Oil, to taste. Toss slightly and top with cucumber and spring onion. Serve immediately.

SHANGHAI-STYLE STICKY PORK BELLY NOODLES

Sticky pork belly is usually a winner for most people—but look out, barbecued pork fans! In my humble opinion, this dish is a more refined version of *char siu* pork. The classic flavors of Shaoxing rice wine and soy build the foundation of this dish, as more fragrant elements are layered using a few different techniques.

Sometimes called red-cooked pork (*hong shao rou*), this is another beloved dish in China, and one of my favorites, too. But instead of the more traditional rice pairing, I've added a noodle variation, similar to one of the most popular dishes we offer at Bumplings—our Mauritian BBQ Pork Noodles.

Before we dive into this, it's important to understand that the secret to many Chinese-style pork dishes is to first blanch the pork briefly. This helps to impart some of that flavor, while cleaning the pork, too.

SERVES 2

Sticky Pork Belly

12.5 oz (350 g) pork belly, skin on

3 tbsp (45 ml) Shaoxing rice wine

1 tbsp (15 ml) light soy sauce

1½ tsp (7.5 ml) dark soy sauce

1 slice fresh ginger

1 star anise

About 2 cups (475 ml) water, plus more if needed

4 to 5 shiitake mushrooms, halved

1 tbsp (21 g) rock sugar

10.5 oz (300 g) thick udon-style Hand-Cut Wheat Noodles (page 155)

Sliced spring onion, for garnish

Make the sticky pork belly: Chop the pork into ¾-inch (2-cm) pieces. Bring a small pot of water to a boil over high heat. Lower the pork pieces into the boiling water and cook for just 1 to 2 minutes. Remove the pork, then drain and rinse it to remove all impurities. Rinse out the pot and discard the water.

Place the pork back in the pot over medium heat, and add the Shaoxing wine, light soy sauce, dark soy sauce, ginger, star anise, plus enough fresh water to cover everything, about 2 cups (475 ml). Bring to a boil, then cover, lower the heat to a simmer, and cook for 30 minutes. Add the shiitake mushrooms and let simmer for another 20 minutes, or until the pork is tender. If the liquid dries out along the way, add a little more water.

Remove the lid and increase the heat to high. Add the rock sugar and let boil for a few minutes, or until the sauce has thickened and become sticky.

Bring a large pot of water to a boil, then cook the noodles for 4 to 5 minutes. Drain and toss with your sticky pork belly. Transfer to a serving platter and garnish with spring onion. Serve immediately.

SPICY CHICKEN TAN TAN RAMEN

A solid ramen takes many, many hours to cook and results in a rich and textural broth, bursting with flavor. This is a bit of a ramen hack, with a few tricks to confer the richness and texture we expect in any good ramen. To give a bit of weight to the broth and tone down the spiciness, the secret ingredient is soy milk. Tried and tested—a best seller at Bumplings during winter—it checks all the boxes for a rich, spicy and delicious broth with some classic Japanese flavors, and can be put together in just a few hours.

SERVES 4

Chicken Mixture

2 tbsp (30 ml) vegetable oil

1 tbsp (15 g) finely minced garlic

1½ tsp (7 g) finely minced fresh ginger

8 oz (225 g) fatty ground chicken

1 tbsp (15 g) doubanjiang chili paste

1 tbsp (15 ml) light soy sauce

1 tbsp (15 ml) Shaoxing rice wine

Tan Tan Soup Base

4 tbsp (15 g) tahini

3 tbsp (45 ml) soy sauce

2 tsp (10 ml) distilled white vinegar

2 tbsp (30 ml) Chinese Chili Oil (page 147)

Soup Stock

2 cups + 2 tbsp (500 ml) chicken stock

1 cup + 2 tsp (250 ml) unsweetened soy milk

17 oz (480 g) thin-cut Hand-Cut Wheat Noodles (page 155)

Bunch of choy sum (Chinese flowering cabbage), trimmed and cut into 2" (5-cm) pieces

Finely sliced spring onion, for serving

Chinese Chili Oil (page 147)

Make the chicken mixture: In a wok, heat the vegetable oil over medium heat. Add the garlic and ginger, and cook, stirring, for 1 minute, or until fragrant. Add the ground chicken and cook, stirring constantly, until cooked through and browned. Add the doubanjiang, light soy sauce and Shaoxing wine and cook, stirring, until the liquid has evaporated. Remove from the heat and transfer to a bowl. Set aside until required.

Make the tan tan soup base: In a bowl, combine all the stock ingredients and stir until well mixed, then set aside.

Make the soup stock: In a small pot, combine all the stock ingredients over medium heat and bring to a boil. Lower the heat to low and keep warm until ready to serve.

Bring a large pot of water to a boil, then cook the noodles for about 3 minutes and drain. Blanch the choy sum separately in the same pot and drain.

To serve, divide the tan tan soup base among four bowls, followed by the noodles and soup stock. Top with the choy sum, cooked chicken and spring onion. Serve immediately, with Chinese chili oil to add to taste.

TWO

EGG NOODLES

Another extremely popular type of noodle is the egg noodle. As the name suggests, it's primarily made of wheat and egg, and is the base noodle for countless favorites around the world.

Growing up, Grandmère made A LOT of egg noodles—likely because this is the main noodle everyone eats in Mauritius—so to this day, it remains one of my go-to noodle choices. One of the most precious memories I have growing up is of eating "longevity noodles" during our family's Chinese New Year celebrations, and Grandmère also makes this for us on birthdays for the extra blessing of a long and happy life.

When a wheat dough is worked, the enzymes that the process activates help break down the starches, which contributes to the development of the dough's texture—as does the gluten in wheat, of course. These specific enzymes are also in egg yolks, so when eggs are worked into a wheat dough, they help break down the starches just that little bit more. Although wheat dough has much more stretch than egg noodles, the fats from the egg yolk and the extra starch breakdown helps give them a much softer feel than standard wheat noodles, with some buttery hints of flavor. This is what makes egg noodles special.

Two of my favorites from this chapter are Chicken Khao Soi Noodles (page 39)—a widely served dish in Thailand—and the absolutely beautiful Fragrant Spring Onion Noodles (page 35) from China. I like all noodles, but thin-cut noodles are up there with the best for me!

Working with egg noodles allows for extra doses of creativity, so I always enjoy making (and eating!) them, and I have absolute confidence you'll love them, too!

LONG LIFE NOODLES

Long life noodles (*yī miàn*)—as the name suggests—are very auspicious noodles usually eaten around the time of Chinese New Year to bring into the new year the wish of a long life for the person eating them. Grandmère still makes these for me to this day, and still tries to make the noodles as long as possible—the longer the noodle, the more longevity you'll have! I've used hand-cut egg noodles here just like Grandmère does; however, traditionally long life noodles are made from a single piece of dough, stretched out to a single unbroken noodle. This is not an easy feat for the beginners, but with a bit of practice and unbroken determination, I'm sure you'll be able to bring some longevity noodles into your own life.

SERVES 4

- 17 oz (480 g) thin-cut Egg Noodles (page 157)
- ½ tsp minced fresh ginger
- ½ tsp minced garlic
- 2 tbsp (30 ml) light soy sauce
- 2 tbsp (30 ml) oyster sauce
- ½ tsp sesame oil
- ¼ tsp freshly ground white pepper
- ½ tsp superfine sugar
- ½ tsp salt
- 2 tbsp (30 ml) water
- 7 oz (200 g) flank steak, sliced thinly
- 2 tbsp (30 ml) vegetable oil, for wok
- 1 onion, sliced
- 2 to 3 spring onions, cut into 2" (5-cm) lengths, white and green parts separated

Bring a large pot of water to a boil, then cook the noodles for about 3 minutes. Drain and set aside.

Make the sauce: In a small bowl, combine the ginger, garlic, light soy sauce, oyster sauce, sesame oil, white pepper, superfine sugar, salt and water, and whisk until well mixed and the sugar has dissolved.

In a separate bowl, marinate the beef by tossing it with 2 tablespoons (30 ml) of the sauce mixture. Set aside, covered, for at least 30 minutes.

In a wok over high heat, heat the vegetable oil. Once hot, add the onion and the white part of the spring onions, and stir-fry for 2 to 3 minutes, or until starting to soften. Add the beef and cook for another 2 minutes, making sure to toss it with a stainless-steel wok spatula, for even cooking. Add the noodles and the remaining sauce mixture and toss well. Cook for another 5 minutes before adding the green part of the spring onions. Toss and cook for another minute before serving.

COLD SESAME NOODLES

This is as simple as it gets—cold egg noodles with an immensely flavorful *bang bang* (sesame-based) sauce.

Although its few ingredients might challenge its status as a meal, this is the kind of dish that pairs perfectly with a side of some Mouthwatering Sichuan Chicken (page 140). Or as a slurpable snack on its own—tasty, creamy, quick and easy.

SERVES 4

Bang Bang Sauce

¼ cup (60 ml) tahini

6 tbsp (90 ml) light soy sauce

4 tbsp (60 ml) Chinese black vinegar

2 tbsp (26 g) superfine sugar

1 cup + 2 tsp (250 ml) Chinese Chili Oil, strained (page 147)

1 clove garlic, minced

½ cup (120 ml) water

17 oz (480 g) thick Egg Noodles (page 157)

Sliced spring onion, for serving

Chopped roasted peanuts, for serving

Roasted white sesame seeds, for serving

Chinese Chili Oil (page 147), for serving

Make the bang bang sauce: In a medium-sized bowl, combine all the sauce ingredients and whisk until well mixed.

Bring a large pot of water to a boil, then cook the noodles for about 3 minutes. Drain and transfer to a large bowl. Drizzle with a generous amount of the bang bang sauce and toss to combine. Divide among four serving bowls and top with the spring onion, roasted peanuts and sesame seeds. Drizzle with some chili oil to finish before serving.

FRAGRANT SPRING ONION NOODLES

Spring onion—or *cong* in Mandarin—is one of the fundamental ingredients for cooking Chinese food, and sees use in many provinces throughout China, including Yunnan, Sichuan and Jiangsu. This brightly flavored ingredient has the performance equivalence of an Oscars Best Supporting Actor winner, and can complement a myriad of dishes, adopting a range of roles and prominence.

Although it's the main component for this recipe, you'll be pleasantly surprised how the savory, sweet and fragrant elements come from one very understated ingredient. This is a nice, easy recipe and an all-time favorite at Bumplings. You might like to add some Japanese Braised Pork Belly (page 143), but I like mine with nothing but the noodles. Although spring onions are traditionally served with wheat noodles, I prefer them with egg noodles (for some extra richness).

Here, you'll cook down the white part of the spring onions first, nice and slow, over low heat, then add the green parts as the white part crisps up. Once the green part is cooked through, it's time to coat your egg noodles in this delicious oil and season well.

SERVES 4

Scant 9 oz (250 g) spring onions
⅓ cup (85 ml) grapeseed oil
3 tbsp (45 ml) light soy sauce
3 tbsp (45 ml) dark soy sauce
5 tsp (20 g) superfine sugar
1 lb (450 g) thin-cut Egg Noodles (page 157)

To prepare the spring onions, cut off the roots and the top inch (2.5 cm) of the dark green tip. Peel the outside layer and rinse thoroughly to remove any grit. Pat dry and cut into 2-inch (5-cm) lengths. Separate the green pieces from the white. Slice each piece of spring onion lengthwise, and working with one piece at a time, place them cut side down. Cut thinly lengthwise to create thin matchsticks. Repeat with all the spring onion pieces.

In a wok over medium heat, heat the grapeseed oil. Add the white part of the spring onions and let them fry slowly. They should maintain a gentle sizzle. Once they turn golden, add the green parts. Gently stir and continue to fry until all the spring onion has become golden brown and crispy. Remove with a strainer and set aside, reserving the oil in the wok.

Add the light soy sauce, dark soy sauce and superfine sugar to the spring onion–flavored oil in the wok, and bring to a gentle boil. Let cook for 5 minutes, then transfer to a bowl and set aside to use as a sauce.

Bring a large pot of water to a boil, then cook the noodles for about 3 minutes. Drain, then divide among 4 serving bowls. Add 1 to 2 tablespoons (15 to 30 ml) of the spring onion sauce to each bowl and top with a handful of fried spring onion pieces. Serve immediately and make sure to toss before eating!

SHANGHAI PORK CHOW MEIN

Chow mein (*chao mian*) is THE ubiquitous menu item found at just about any standard Chinese restaurant. Chow mein has umpteen versions, but today we're going to be looking at the good old Shanghai-style chow mein. Most Westerners will be familiar with this thicker egg noodle, which normally can be found in your neighborhood supermarket; at Asian grocers, they are known as Hokkien noodles.

Unlike the Shanghai-Style Sticky Pork Belly Noodles (page 16), which is rich and thick, this features a lighter and more savory sauce, without compromising on the flavor of the pork.

SERVES 4

Marinated Pork

8 oz (220 g) pork shoulder, sliced into thin strips

1 tsp cornstarch

1 tsp light soy sauce

½ tsp dark soy sauce

1 tsp Shaoxing rice wine

½ tsp superfine sugar

17 oz (480 g) thick Egg Noodles (page 157)

To Stir-Fry

Vegetable oil, for wok

6 dried shiitake mushrooms, soaked in water, then drained and sliced

2 oz (60 g) dried black fungus, soaked in water, then drained and cut into 1¼" (3-cm) pieces

1 tsp minced fresh ginger

1 tbsp (15 ml) oyster sauce

1½ tsp (8 ml) light soy sauce

1½ tsp (8 ml) dark soy sauce

½ tsp superfine sugar

Bunch of kailan (Chinese broccoli), washed and trimmed

Finely chopped chives, for serving

Marinate the pork: In a medium-sized bowl, combine the pork, cornstarch, light soy sauce, dark soy sauce, Shaoxing wine and superfine sugar, and mix well. Set aside, covered, to marinate for at least 30 minutes.

When ready to cook, bring a large pot of water to a boil, then cook the noodles for about 3 minutes, or until just cooked through. Drain, then set aside until required.

In a wok over high heat, heat 2 tablespoons (30 ml) of vegetable oil. When hot, add the marinated pork and stir-fry until browned, about 5 minutes. Remove the pork from the wok and set aside. Add another 2 tablespoons (30 ml) of vegetable oil to the wok. When hot, add the shiitake mushrooms, black fungus and ginger. Stir-fry for 2 to 3 minutes before adding the noodles. Add the oyster sauce, light soy sauce, dark soy sauce, superfine sugar and *kailan* and toss, cooking for another 2 to 3 minutes before serving. Top with chopped chives.

CHICKEN KHAO SOI NOODLES

This classic Thai dish is a standout and comes from northern Thailand, which is home to some of the spiciest foods with a rich complexity of flavors. *Khao soi* in and of itself isn't super spicy on the Scoville scale, but the curried soup base is laden with some strong spices, including turmeric, cumin and coriander.

One of the other things I love about a traditional khao soi is its doubling down on the noodles—some fried egg noodles sprinkled on top are a MUST to contrast with the soft egg noodles in the curried soup base.

SERVES 4

Khao Soi Paste

2 Thai red chiles

2 medium-sized shallots, roughly chopped

4 cloves garlic

2 tbsp (12 g) diced fresh ginger

2 tbsp (12 g) diced fresh turmeric

Small handful of fresh cilantro stems and root

2 tsp (4 g) ground coriander

1 tsp ground cardamom

1 tsp curry powder

2 tbsp (30 g) shrimp paste

Soup

2 tbsp (30 ml) vegetable oil

1 lb (450 g) boneless chicken thighs

2 tbsp (15 g) red curry paste

4¼ cups (1 L) chicken stock

2 tsp (6 g) palm sugar

1 (13.5-oz [400-ml]) can coconut milk

3 tbsp (45 ml) Asian fish sauce

Salt (optional)

14 oz (400 g) thin-cut Egg Noodles (page 157)

Scant 2 oz (50 g) thin-cut Egg Noodles, deep-fried (page 157)

2 shallots, thinly sliced

2 limes, cut into wedges

3.5 oz (100 g) pickled mustard greens, chopped

Fresh cilantro, for serving

Mung bean sprouts, for serving

Make the khao soi paste: In a food processor, combine all the paste ingredients and blitz until smooth. Transfer to a small bowl and set aside until required.

Make the soup: In a wok over high heat, heat the vegetable oil. Once hot, add the chicken and stir-fry until golden brown, about 5 minutes. Remove the chicken and set aside. Add the khao soi paste to the wok and cook, stirring, for 3 minutes. Add the red curry paste, chicken stock and palm sugar, and bring to a boil. Lower the heat and add the coconut milk and fish sauce. Add back the chicken and let simmer for another 5 to 10 minutes. Taste and season with salt, if required.

Bring a large pot of water to a boil and cook the noodles for about 3 minutes, or until just cooked through. Drain, then divide among four serving bowls. Ladle the hot khao soi soup and chicken over the cooked noodles. Top with the deep-fried noodles, sliced shallots, lime wedges, pickled mustard greens, cilantro and mung bean sprouts. Serve immediately.

THREE

RICE NOODLES

A younger sibling to wheat noodles, rice noodles have been thought to have originated in south China as rice grew plentifully in that region.

On their own, rice noodles may have an almost nonexistent taste, which can present some challenges when not used correctly, but I think this makes them the perfect carrier for additional flavors—especially the ones described in this chapter.

Some of the most fantastic rice noodle dishes I've tasted come from Southeast Asia. In Vietnam and Thailand, for example, rice noodles tend to accompany delicious broths (e.g., a classic Vietnamese *pho*), or can be made into more refreshing, vibrant dishes (e.g., the traditional Thai glass noodle salad) that are ideal in a hot and humid climate.

While wheat noodles can be springy and doughy, and egg noodles are noticeably softer, rice noodles, when produced and cooked correctly, are delicate with a very velvety mouthfeel. This is because rice is almost entirely devoid of protein—which can give firmness to the noodles—but is instead full of carbs (starch) that gelatinize upon cooking.

Ultrathin rice vermicelli is probably one of the best-known forms of this noodle, but the additional cooking step and drying out that happens in commercial vermicelli production can make it a bit firmer and more brittle than desired. Fresh rice noodles—as we'll be making in this chapter—couldn't be more different.

Rice noodles start off with more of a batter than a dough and are generally cooked in two different ways: extruded into a pot of boiling water or steamed in sheets. If you don't own a noodle press or extruder (I don't!), you can make do by drizzling thin strands of rice noodle batter into a pot of boiling water, using a piping bag (or even just a sandwich bag with a tiny cut in the corner). Have a set of tongs at the ready, because they cook and set almost upon impact. The steamed rice noodle sheets are incredibly versatile and can be cut into any shape or size after cooking, or simply left as a glorious silky sheet.

Other than it being conventionally cooked as a grain, rice can be used in a variety of ways and, as we'll describe, can produce a wonderful variety of noodles, noodles which also complement many of the flavors in this book.

THAI SPICY PORK VERMICELLI

Hot tip: Instead of just rehydrating your vermicelli and mixing it into a broth, dress your noodles as you would a salad and let them soak up the sauce. In a broth, they can become saturated, soggy and break apart. In this Thai-style recipe, that's not gonna happen. Although they're initially bland, they're really just a blank canvas. All the hallmark flavors of Thai cuisine are begging to add some color and vibrancy to these noodles—lime, fish sauce, cilantro and lots of chile.

SERVES 2 TO 3

Salad Dressing

3 tbsp (45 ml) Asian fish sauce

3 tbsp (45 ml) lime juice

2 tbsp (30 g) palm sugar

1 tbsp (10 g) finely minced garlic

3 to 5 Thai red chiles, finely minced

Pinch of salt

5.5 oz (150 g) ground pork

5.5 oz (150 g) raw prawn tails, peeled

1 to 2 shallots, thinly sliced

1 cup (150 g) halved cherry tomatoes

Handful of cilantro, chopped

Handful of fresh mint leaves, chopped

⅔ cup (97 g) roasted peanuts, chopped, divided

7 oz (200 g) Thin Rice Noodles, cooked (page 159)

Make the salad dressing: In a small bowl, combine all the dressing ingredients and whisk well. Set aside until required.

Place a medium-sized pot filled with water over high heat. Once boiling, submerge the ground pork, using a sieve, and agitate it until the pork is cooked through and broken into smaller pieces, about 6 to 8 minutes. Remove, drain and transfer to a large bowl. Do the same for the raw prawn tails, about 6 to 8 minutes. Add the shallots, tomatoes, cilantro, mint leaves, half of the peanuts, the cooked rice noodles and dressing to the bowl. Toss gently until well combined and transfer to your serving bowl. Top with the remaining peanuts and enjoy.

LEMONGRASS BEEF NOODLE SALAD

I can appreciate a well-made meal slaved over for many hours, but I can also appreciate something that gets slapped together in minimal time, with maximum taste. Enter stage left: lemongrass beef noodle salad. This Vietnamese-inspired dish uses beef marinated in a simple lemongrass and soy-heavy sauce, tossed through with fresh herbs, steamed rice noodles and a tangy-spicy Vietnamese dressing. Marinating time is not required, but going hard on the dressing definitely is.

SERVES 4

Marinated Beef

1 lb (450 g) flank steak, thinly sliced

4 tbsp (30 g) finely minced fresh lemongrass

6 cloves garlic, finely minced

6 tbsp (30 g) finely minced fresh ginger

2 tbsp (30 ml) Asian fish sauce

1 tbsp (15 ml) oyster sauce

2 tbsp (26 g) superfine sugar

2 tbsp (30 ml) vegetable oil

Nuoc Cham Sauce

Scant ⅔ cup (135 ml) boiling water

3 tbsp (39 g) granulated sugar

3 tbsp (45 ml) fresh lime juice

3 tbsp (45 ml) Asian fish sauce

1 clove garlic, minced

1 small red chile, finely sliced

Scant 9 oz (250 g) Thin Rice Noodles (page 159), cooked

Large handful of fresh Thai basil leaves, divided

Large handful of fresh mint leaves, divided

A large handful of fresh cilantro, roughly chopped, divided

½ cucumber, sliced into rounds

1 carrot, julienned

Chopped roasted peanuts, for serving

Marinate the beef: In a medium-sized bowl, combine the flank steak, lemongrass, garlic, ginger, fish sauce, oyster sauce, superfine sugar and vegetable oil, then massage the beef with your hands until all its surfaces are covered with the mixture. Cover with plastic wrap and set aside, refrigerated, to marinate for at least 4 hours, or ideally overnight.

Make the *nuoc cham* sauce: In a small bowl, combine the boiling hot water and granulated sugar, and stir until the sugar has dissolved. Add the remaining nuoc cham sauce ingredients and mix until well incorporated. Taste and adjust the seasoning as required.

Grill the marinated steak on a barbecue hot plate or on an oiled rack over charcoal, for about 2 minutes on each side, or until lightly charred and cooked through. Remove from the heat and keep warm.

To serve, in a large bowl, combine the cooked noodles with half of the Thai basil, mint and cilantro and half of the nuoc cham. Toss gently and divide among four serving bowls. Top with the grilled steak, cucumber, carrot, remaining Thai basil, mint and cilantro, and the roasted peanuts. Drizzle with more nuoc cham, if desired.

PEANUT RICE NOODLE ROLLS

At Bumplings, sesame sauce comes standard in many of our dishes. Why not? It's delicious.

So, one day, I made some steamed rice flour sheets, rolled them up, cut them into smaller rolls and threw some sesame sauce on top—and a star was born.

Since its inception, I've done a few modifications and ended up with a bit of a Southeast Asian flavor, with a peanut sauce, a fresh burst of lime and some chile (of course!). Thick-cut rice flour noodle rolls, with a nice bouncy texture—the perfect vehicle for a peanutty flavor.

SERVES 4

Rice Noodle Rolls

¾ cup + 1 tsp (123 g) rice flour

⅓ cup + 1 tsp (48 g) tapioca starch

1½ cups + 4 tsp (375 ml) water

Vegetable oil spray

To Serve

Peanut Sauce (page 148)

Chinese Chili Oil (page 147)

Sliced spring onion

Chopped roasted peanuts

1 lime, quartered

Make the rice noodle rolls: In a large liquid measuring cup, combine the rice flour, tapioca starch and water, and whisk until a smooth batter is formed.

Place a large steamer basket in your wok over high heat and add water to the wok until the water line is 1 inch (2.5 cm) below the bottom of the steamer. Once the water is boiling, lower the heat to medium.

Select a pizza pan or heatproof plate that fits into your steamer basket, and spray it lightly with vegetable oil. Pour a thin layer of batter onto the oiled pan, swirling if needed to spread evenly. Place the pan in the steamer basket, cover and steam for 2 to 3 minutes, or until the rice noodle skin becomes translucent. Remove the pan from the steamer and let cool slightly before rolling the noodle tightly into a long log. Set aside on an oiled baking sheet and repeat the process with the remaining batter. Slice the logs into 1½- to 2-inch (4- to 5-cm) lengths and divide among four serving bowls. Drizzle generously with peanut sauce and a little Chinese chili oil. Top with spring onion and roasted peanuts, with a wedge of lime on the side, before serving.

STEAMED PRAWN RICE NOODLE ROLLS

Sometimes called rice flour rolls, rice noodle rolls (*cheung fun*) are an undisputed Cantonese dim sum classic. Rice noodle rolls can be filled with any protein of choice, but prawn just does it for me. Next time you're having dim sum (and if it's available), do yourself a favor and have the rice noodle rolls with the deep-fried prawn donut inside—it is next-level heavenly. However, while it does elevate the dish, the donut is also the next-level to cook, so I've excluded it from this recipe. If you're keen to add them, you can probably still find them at some Asian grocery stores, but this dish tastes amazing without them, too! Squishy rice noodles, crunchy prawn flesh, salty soy dressing—this dim sum classic is all about the texture.

SERVES 2

Marinated Prawns

Scant 9 oz (250 g) prawn tails, peeled

½ tsp minced fresh ginger

½ tsp cornstarch

Dash of sesame oil

Pinch of salt

Pinch of freshly ground white pepper

Sweet Soy Sauce

2 tbsp + 2 tsp (40 ml) light soy sauce

2 tsp (10 ml) dark soy sauce

2 tsp (10 ml) oyster sauce

2 tbsp (26 g) superfine sugar

⅓ cup + 1 tsp (85 ml) water

Pinch of salt

Rice Noodle Rolls

¾ cup + 1 tsp (123 g) rice flour

⅓ cup + 1 tsp (48 g) tapioca starch

1½ cups + 4 tsp (375 ml) water

Vegetable oil spray

2 spring onions, green part only, sliced

Marinate the prawns: In a bowl, combine the prawn tails, ginger, cornstarch, sesame oil, salt and white pepper, and toss until mixed. Cover with plastic wrap and refrigerate to marinate for 1 hour.

Make the sweet soy sauce: In a small pot over medium heat, combine all the sauce ingredients. Mix well and cook for 2 to 3 minutes, or until the sauce starts to bubble. Remove from the heat and transfer to a large liquid measuring cup.

Make the rice noodle rolls: In a separate large measuring cup, combine the rice flour, tapioca starch and water, and whisk until a smooth batter is formed.

Place a large steamer basket in your wok over high heat and add water to the wok until the water line is 1 inch (2.5 cm) below the bottom of the steamer. Once the water is boiling, lower the heat to medium.

Place the marinated prawns on a pizza pan or heatproof plate that fits into your steamer basket, cover and steam until cooked through, 5 to 10 minutes. Remove from the steamer and set aside.

Fit a separate round pan into your steamer and spray lightly with vegetable oil spray. Pour on a thin layer of batter, swirling if needed to spread evenly, then sprinkle lightly with some spring onion. Cover and steam for 2 to 3 minutes, or until the rice noodle skin becomes translucent. Remove from the steamer and let cool slightly. Line the middle of the round rice noodle sheet with three to five steamed prawns, and roll the sheet over to enclose the prawns and form a tube. Transfer to your serving dish and repeat with remaining batter and prawns. Serve immediately with the sweet soy drizzled on top.

GRANDMÈRE'S CHICKEN VERMICELLI

Every family has its own chicken soup. This is my family's. Grandmère's soup is very Mauritian, using a combination of elements from French and Chinese cooking. The stock has accents of spring onion, celery and carrot (known as a mirepoix), giving it an herbal and slightly sweet edge, but it is a classic Asian-style bone broth that's boosted with some dried shiitake. Bones are best for any stock—It's amazing how much flavor can be pulled out of so little meat.

FYI: Grandmère is stoked to make it into both of my cookbooks.

SERVES 4

---

2 tbsp (30 ml) vegetable oil

17.5 oz (500 g) chicken drumettes and wings, cut in half

Salt

2 spring onions, white parts only

2 large carrots, cut into 1¼" (2-cm) pieces

3 celery ribs, cut into 1¼" (2-cm) pieces

6 dried shiitake mushrooms, soaked in water, then drained and sliced

4 cloves garlic, sliced

2 tbsp (30 ml) light soy sauce

4 slices fresh ginger

8 cups (2 L) water

½ tsp freshly ground white pepper

8 oz (225 g) Thin Rice Noodles (page 159)

Chopped spring onion, for garnish

Place a large pot over medium heat and heat the vegetable oil. Once hot, add the chicken pieces and a pinch of salt. Rotate the chicken pieces until golden brown on all sides, 6 to 8 minutes. Add the spring onion white parts, carrots, celery, shiitake mushrooms, garlic, light soy sauce and ginger. Cover with the water, stir and bring to a boil. Once boiling, lower the heat to a simmer and cook for 25 to 30 minutes, or until the chicken is tender. Remove the slices of ginger, add the white pepper and salt to taste, then stir well to mix. Add the rice noodles and mix gently before serving. Garnish with spring onion.

SIZZLING BEEF CHOW FUN

"Sizzling beef" conjures up images of that very specific shallow cast-iron dish on the wooden holder, hissing loudly and drawing everyone's gaze in the restaurant on the way over to the table. *Chow fun* is like a sibling of chow mein and arguably better known—many different Asian cultures have their signature version. Sometimes called *ho fun*, it's a simplification of the dish, just referring to the fettuccine-sized rice noodles used in it.

Marinate far in advance (one day) for maximum flavor, and have all elements ready to go before you start this cook—it will only take a minute or two of actual cooking time (you guessed it, it's a stir-fry). You, too, can conjure up these memories of sizzling beef in your own kitchen and without that very special serving dish—but if the wok isn't hot, the beef won't sizzle!

SERVES 4

Marinated Beef

1 lb (450 g) flank steak, sliced into thin strips

2 tsp (5 g) cornstarch

1 tbsp (15 ml) oyster sauce

1 tbsp (15 ml) light soy sauce

1 tsp superfine sugar

Pinch of freshly ground white pepper

To Stir-Fry

Vegetable oil, for wok

6 thin slices fresh ginger

6 spring onions, sliced diagonally

21 oz (600 g) Rice Noodle Sheets, freshly cooked (page 158)

3 tbsp (45 ml) Shaoxing rice wine

1 tsp sesame oil

2 tbsp (30 ml) dark soy sauce

4 tbsp (60 ml) light soy sauce

½ tsp superfine sugar

Pinch of freshly ground white pepper

Salt

1 cup (100 g) mung bean sprouts

Marinate the beef: In a medium-sized bowl, combine the flank steak, cornstarch, oyster sauce, light soy sauce, superfine sugar and white pepper, and toss until well combined. Cover with plastic wrap and refrigerate to marinate for about 1 hour or ideally overnight. Remove from the fridge 30 minutes before you are ready to cook.

In a wok over high heat, heat 2 tablespoons (30 ml) of vegetable oil. When hot, add the marinated beef and cook, tossing until golden brown, about 5 minutes. Remove the beef from the wok and set aside. Place the wok back over high heat and add 1 tablespoon (15 ml) of vegetable oil. Add the ginger, followed by the spring onions. Toss for about 1 minute before adding the cooked rice noodles (see note). Spread them evenly across the wok and drizzle with the Shaoxing wine. Stir-fry for about 1 minute. Add the sesame oil, dark soy sauce, light soy sauce, superfine sugar, ground white pepper and salt to taste, and add back the cooked beef. Stir-fry, tossing to ensure everything is well combined. Add the mung bean sprouts and toss for about 30 seconds before removing from the heat and serving.

NOTE:

- If the rice noodles are stuck together, blanch briefly by dropping them into boiling water for 2 minutes, before dropping into ice water to help separate them. Make sure to drain well before adding to your wok to cook.

SPICY PRAWN CHAR KWAY TEOW

Char kway teow—sometimes comparable to *pad see ew*—are your classic thick-cut stir-fried rice noodles, and a staple at most Singaporean or Malaysian-style restaurants. Two of the most important elements for a good char kway teow: great sauce and a solid "char" flavor. The "char" relates to the smokiness of the dish, and here are a few pointers for how you can get that delicious edge into your kway teow that you'd taste from a street vendor:

Once your rice noodles are good to go, cook them in the wok first for a good amount of time before you add the sauce and prawns. It might be more time consuming, but don't crowd the wok; cook your noodles in batches. Next, a well-seasoned wok conducts heat quickly, but if you don't have one, make sure your oil is smoking before you drop in the noodles. Finally, burning off a little bit of dark soy sauce and sweet soy sauce in the wok before you cook your noodles in it will do wonders for the "char."

SERVES 4

Spicy Sauce

1 tbsp + 2 tsp (25 ml) The OG Chili Sauce (page 148), plus more for serving

1 tbsp + 2 tsp (25 ml) dark soy sauce

4 tsp (20 ml) light soy sauce

2 tsp (10 ml) oyster sauce

4 tsp (20 ml) sweet soy sauce

Vegetable oil, for wok

2 cloves garlic, finely chopped

20 prawn tails, peeled

1 Chinese sausage, thinly sliced on the diagonal

2 large eggs, whisked

17.5 oz (500 g) Rice Noodle Sheets, freshly cooked (page 158)

2 cups (200 g) mung bean sprouts

1 bunch garlic chives, cut into 1" (2.5-cm) lengths

Make the spicy sauce: In a small bowl, combine all the spicy sauce ingredients and set aside until required

In a wok over high heat, heat 2 tablespoons (30 ml) of vegetable oil. When hot, add the garlic and stir-fry for about 30 seconds, or until fragrant. Add the prawn tails and stir-fry until cooked, about 2 minutes. Remove from the wok and set aside. Add the Chinese sausage to the hot wok and cook for 2 to 3 minutes, or until lightly crisp. Remove from the wok and set aside.

Keeping the wok on high heat, add another tablespoon (15 ml) of oil. Add the whisked eggs and swirl around the wok to cover as much surface area as possible. After 2 minutes, flip the omelet and cook for another 2 minutes. Slide the omelet onto a chopping board and slice into ¾-inch (2-cm) shreds.

To bring everything together, add 1 tablespoon (15 ml) of vegetable oil to the wok and add the cooked flat rice noodles. Toss for about 30 seconds. Add back the prawns, Chinese sausage and egg shreds. Now, add the mung bean sprouts, garlic chives and the spicy sauce. Toss gently to combine, before transferring to your serving dish. Serve with extra chili sauce as desired.

FOUR

CRYSTAL CLEAR NOODLES

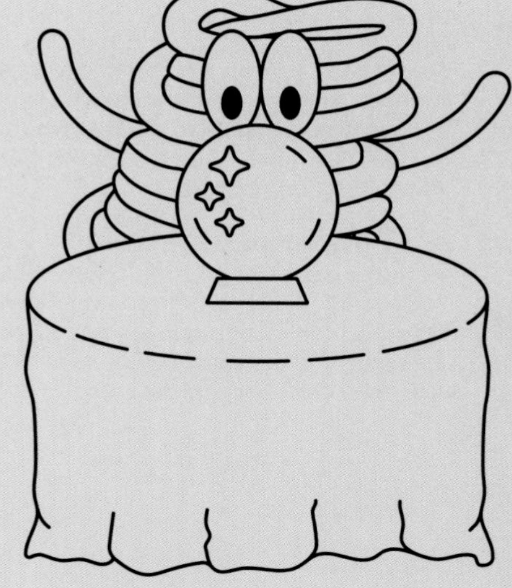

Given that rice can be used in a multitude of ways in its flour form, why shouldn't that extend to other rich sources of carbs? This is where things really start to get interesting!

The noodles in this chapter are made from some very different kinds of starches that the average household might not have on hand, such as potato starch, sweet potato starch and mung bean starch. Fascinatingly, these three types of starch have one thing in common: When cooked in starch form, they give a ghostly, semi-translucent appearance—hence, crystal clear noodles.

Crystal clear noodles are virtually protein-free and made entirely of starch, and if you've been following on from the previous chapter, it's a fair assessment that crystal noodles share many similarities with rice noodles. Crystal clear noodles are clearly (see what I did there) characterized by their translucency but as another point of difference, crystal clear noodles are more jellylike than rice noodles are, with a slippery, squishy and stretchy texture.

With similar principles to the rice flour noodles (in both making the batter and cooking), once you've had a go at rice flour noodles, then this should be the next stop.

Within the crystal clear noodle category, sweet potato noodles are some of my all-time favorites and have a remarkable stretch. Despite sweet potato having quite a strong and characteristic sweet taste, in starch form it is much more toned down and incredibly versatile. This makes such noodles a perfect match for more punchy and intense dishes, such as Sichuan Handmade Potato Noodles (Suān La Fén) (page 67).

If you're up to getting a little out of your comfort zone to explore some treasured dishes from different cultures, and are a fellow lover of more glutinous and silky textures—this is the chapter for you!

KOREAN BEEF JAPCHAE

Japchae is a staple at most Korean restaurants. Served warm or even slightly cool, this sesame-centered noodle dish has a slightly sweet sauce balanced by delicious savory beef, with layers of texture.

Made with (purple) sweet potato starch, these noodles get a mesmerizing translucent aspect when cooked. In comparison to rice vermicelli, sweet potato noodles have a slight jellyish and stretchy texture that I absolutely love.

SERVES 4

---

1 lb (450 g) Sweet Potato Noodles (page 160)

Vegetable oil, for wok

2 lb (900 g) boneless beef rib eye, sliced into strips

4 tbsp (60 ml) sesame oil, divided

6 tbsp (90 ml) light soy sauce, divided

3 tbsp (15 g) light brown sugar, divided

Freshly ground black pepper

3 carrots, julienned

1 white onion, thinly sliced

6 spring onions, cut into 2" (5-cm) lengths, white and green parts separated

6 cloves garlic, minced

2 cups (60 g) spinach

Toasted white sesame seeds, for garnish

2 long red chiles, sliced for garnish

Bring a large pot of water to a boil, then cook the noodles for about 5 minutes, or until just cooked through. Drain, transfer to a large bowl and set aside until required.

In a wok over high heat, heat 1 tablespoon (15 ml) of vegetable oil. Carefully place the beef in the wok and stir until all its edges are starting to sear, 2 to 3 minutes. Season with 2 tablespoons (30 ml) of the sesame oil, 3 tablespoons (45 ml) of the light soy sauce, 1½ tablespoons (8 g) of the brown sugar and a pinch of black pepper. Continue to cook, tossing, until golden brown, about 5 minutes. Remove from the heat and transfer to the bowl with your noodles.

Place the wok back over high heat and add another tablespoon (15 ml) of vegetable oil. Add the carrots, onion and the white parts of the spring onions. While stirring, add the remaining 2 tablespoons (30 ml) of sesame oil, 3 tablespoons (45 ml) of light soy sauce, 1½ tablespoons (8 g) of brown sugar and a pinch of black pepper. When the veggies start to soften, add the garlic and the green parts of the spring onions. Cook for 2 to 3 minutes, or until softened, then add the spinach. Turn off the heat and add the noodles and beef. Toss until well combined, then transfer to a serving platter. Sprinkle with some toasted white sesame seeds and red chile, and serve.

ANTS CLIMBING A TREE VERMICELLI

"Ants climbing a tree" (*ma yi shang shu*) is a very famous Sichuanese dish with a unique name. Visual elements of this dish resemble a tree (the mung bean vermicelli), the tree's leaves (the spring onion) and the ants climbing the tree (the flecks of ground pork). Rest assured, there are no actual ants in this dish! Unless you choose to include them.

Composed of ground pork, very thin mung bean glass noodles and spring onions with a spicy salty bean paste (don't go too heavy on the spices, or you might find yourself climbing the walls), this dish doesn't just taste great, it's a fun one to create, too, and will certainly be a talking point at the table.

SERVES 2

1 tbsp (15 ml) vegetable oil

1 tbsp (5 g) finely minced fresh ginger

1 tbsp (15 g) doubanjiang chili paste

3.5 oz (100 g) fatty ground pork

1 cup + 2 tsp (250 ml) chicken stock

½ tsp superfine sugar

Pinch of freshly ground white pepper

1 tsp dark soy sauce

2 tsp (10 ml) light soy sauce

3.5 oz (100 g) Mung Bean (Jelly) Noodles, freshly cooked (page 161)

¼ cup (25 g) finely sliced spring onion

2 cloves garlic, minced

1 long red chile, minced

Place a wok over medium heat and heat the vegetable oil. When hot, add the ginger and stir for 1 to 2 minutes, or until fragrant. Add the doubanjiang chili paste and let cook for another 1 to 2 minutes, then add the ground pork. Cook, stirring, until the pork is cooked through and golden brown, about 3 to 5 minutes. Add the chicken stock, superfine sugar, white pepper, dark soy sauce and light soy sauce. Continue to cook, stirring, and when boiling, add the cooked mung bean noodles, spring onion, garlic and red chile. Toss until well combined and serve immediately.

STEAMED SCALLOPS WITH GLASS NOODLES

This is my version of a tasty Cantonese appetizer. The scallop gets removed from its shell and taken aside to be steamed. Meanwhile, that shell gets repurposed as a serving plate. All the usual suspects come to play (ginger, spring onion, soy) to dress up the mung bean noodles; mount them on top of the shells in a little nest, with the steamed scallops on top to finish off.

SERVES 4

1 tbsp (15 ml) vegetable oil

3 cloves garlic, minced

1 spring onion, minced, for garnish

8 scallops in their shell

3.5 oz (100 g) Mung Bean (Jelly) Noodles (page 161), freshly cooked

Fresh cilantro leaves, for serving

Sauce

2 tbsp (10 g) minced fresh ginger

1 clove garlic, minced

1 tbsp (1 g) chopped fresh cilantro

2 tbsp (30 ml) light soy sauce

1 tbsp (15 ml) dark soy sauce

1 tsp superfine sugar

In a small skillet over medium heat, heat the vegetable oil. When hot, add the garlic and spring onion and cook, stirring, for 2 to 3 minutes, or until golden and fragrant. Remove from the heat and set aside to cool.

Remove the scallops from their shells and set aside. Divide and place the cooked mung bean noodles evenly on top of each scallop shell. Place the scallops on the beds of noodles

Make the sauce: In a liquid measuring cup, mix together all the sauce ingredients and pour over the scallops.

Line a bamboo steamer by placing your steamer basket on a sheet of parchment paper. Trace around the basket with a pencil and cut with scissors. Place the cutout into the basket and carefully poke holes with a knife to allow for steam to come through. Place your basket in a wok. Pour enough water into the wok until the water line is 1 inch (2.5 cm) below the bottom of the steamer. Place over high heat.

Place scallops 1 inch (2.5 cm) apart in the steamer basket. Steam in batches for 2 to 4 minutes, or until cooked through.

Pour the garlic and spring onion mixture over the steamed scallops and serve immediately, garnished with cilantro leaves.

SOUR MUSTARD GREEN NOODLE STEW

Although the Yunnan province in China's south is primarily about sour flavors, this sour mustard green glass noodle stew comes from the colder northeast of China. This dish takes diners on a tasty journey, presenting hints of sweetness, followed by the familiar embrace from the savory rich pork broth, with gentle pecks from the Sichuan peppercorns and a sour edge from the mustard greens to round off this symphony of flavors.

SERVES 4

Soup Base

1 lb (450 g) pork ribs

1 tbsp (15 ml) Shaoxing rice wine

2 slices fresh ginger

1 spring onion, white part only

Pinch of salt

2 cups + 2 tbsp (500 ml) water

Pork Dipping Sauce

1 tbsp (15 ml) Chinese Chili Oil (page 147)

2 tbsp (30 ml) light soy sauce

½ tsp superfine sugar

1 clove garlic, finely minced

1 tbsp (15 ml) vegetable oil

2 slices fresh ginger

2 spring onions, sliced, white and green parts separated

7 oz (200 g) sour mustard greens (*suan cai*), rinsed and sliced

1 tbsp (15 ml) oyster sauce

½ cup + 1 tsp (125 ml) chicken stock

Pinch of freshly ground white pepper

7 oz (200 g) Sweet Potato Noodles (page 160), freshly cooked

Salt

Make the soup base: Place a large pot over medium heat and fill with the pork ribs, Shaoxing wine, ginger, spring onion, salt and water. Cover and bring to a boil, then lower the heat to a simmer. Let cook for about 15 minutes on low heat, then turn off the heat, remove the spring onion and ginger, and leave to sit covered.

Make the pork dipping sauce: In a small bowl, combine all the sauce ingredients and stir well. Set aside until required.

In a large pot over medium heat, heat the vegetable oil. When hot, add the ginger, white part of the spring onions and sour mustard greens. Cook, stirring, for about 5 minutes. Add the pork ribs and all of their cooking liquid, oyster sauce, chicken stock and white pepper. Bring to a boil, then lower the heat to a low simmer. Let cook for 15 minutes. Add the cooked sweet potato noodles and stir gently. Season with salt as desired, then serve, garnishing with the green part of the spring onions and the pork dipping sauce on the side.

SICHUAN HANDMADE POTATO NOODLES (SUĀN LA FÉN)

Suān la fén is sometimes called hot and sour glass noodle soup. As you may be aware, glass noodles can be made from a variety of different starches or bases, but all have a crystal clear appearance in common. My version of this crystal noodle dish uses a potato starch base.

The Sichuan province is well known for incredibly spicy food—in particular *mala* food. The word "mala" means "spicy and numbing," and even though there's no mala seasoning in this, it is definitely both spicy and numbing.

SERVES 2

1 tbsp (15 ml) vegetable oil

2 tbsp (40 g) peanuts

2 cups + 2 tbsp (500 ml) chicken stock

7 oz (200 g) Sweet Potato Noodles (page 160), freshly cooked

⅓ cup + 2 tsp (100 g) Chunky Noodle Salsa (page 152)

¼ cup (50 g) pickled mustard greens, finely chopped

Small handful of fresh cilantro, sliced

1 spring onion, sliced

In a small skillet over medium heat, heat the vegetable oil. When hot, add the peanuts and cook, stirring, until golden brown. Remove from the heat.

In a small pot over high heat, heat the chicken stock. When the stock comes to a boil, divide the cooked sweet potato noodles evenly between two serving bowls, then divide the noodle salsa between the bowls. Pour the hot chicken broth over each bowl and top with the fried peanuts, pickled mustard greens, cilantro and spring onion. Serve immediately.

FRAGRANT SEAFOOD BROTH WITH MUNG BEAN NOODLES

The extensive use of beans in China and much of the East has produced endless permutations and applications of this versatile ingredient. And mung bean is certainly one of the stars. To name just a few applications, mung bean can be salted and fermented, made into a sauce, used as a sweet bean filling in cakes and desserts and processed into a starch.

Like sweet potato noodles, mung bean starch goes see-through upon cooking, giving these noodles a ghostly appearance. But don't be afraid! Paired with this simple seafood broth, the only thing you'd be afraid of is not having enough!

SERVES 4

Fragrant Soup Paste

4½ tbsp (30 g) peeled and chopped fresh ginger

Scant 2 tbsp (10 g) peeled and chopped fresh turmeric

2 lemongrass stalks, white parts only, chopped

2 shallots, peeled, chopped

4 cloves garlic, chopped

1 long red chile

Zest of 1 lime

1 tbsp (15 ml) vegetable oil

1 tbsp (15 ml) vegetable oil

1 tbsp (16 g) tomato paste

1 cup + 2 tsp (250 ml) coconut cream

2 cups + 2 tbsp (500 ml) fish stock

4 tbsp (60 ml) Asian fish sauce

1 tbsp (15 g) palm sugar

7 oz (200 g) prawn tails

7 oz (200 g) mussels

7 oz (200 g) white fish filets, cut into 2" (5-cm) pieces

Juice of 1 lime

14 oz (400 g) Mung Bean (Jelly) Noodles (page 161), freshly cooked

To Serve

Fresh Thai basil leaves

Fresh cilantro leaves

Handful of mung bean sprouts

Make the fragrant soup paste: In a food processor, combine all the soup paste ingredients and blitz until a paste is formed.

In a large, deep saucepan over medium heat, heat the vegetable oil. When hot, add the fragrant soup paste and cook, stirring until fragrant, 2 to 3 minutes. Add the tomato paste, coconut cream, fish stock, fish sauce and palm sugar, and bring to a boil. Lower the heat and simmer for 15 minutes. If it is a little thick, add some additional fish stock. Taste and adjust the seasoning with fish sauce or palm sugar. When you're happy, add the prawns and let cook for 2 to 3 minutes. Add the mussels and fish, then cook for another 2 to 3 minutes, or until all the seafood is just cooked through. Squeeze in the lime juice and stir gently until combined.

To serve, divide the cooked mung bean noodles among four serving bowls. Top with the seafood soup and garnish with Thai basil, cilantro and mung bean sprouts.

FIVE

NOODLE SOUPS

At this point, I've covered the major kinds of noodles. The next progression is to pair some of the types of noodles to a range of soup bases and styles. If you've got a pressure cooker, you'll get a lot of bang for your buck out of this chapter, as this will speed up your cooking time even more. But it's certainly not necessary, as a nice big stockpot works great, too.

Noodle soups are often considered a comfort food—and they certainly are. They also tick a few other boxes for me, especially in the effort and mess criteria.

Typically, I don't make very many Western-style stock-based soups, or throw in a lot of vegetables with the meat. I prefer keeping the stock less complex before I add other elements, such as noodles. This personal preference probably comes from being used to cleaner flavors at home and throughout my childhood. In my experience, the best soups are all about getting the most out of what you put in, not how many different things you put in. There are a few exceptions to this rule in the next few pages, but in general, that's a key guiding principle to cooking.

As such, some of the soups I pair with noodles may appear to have very simple bases with just a few ingredients and you may want to add some extra things, but resist the urge if you can. The intention is to spend more time developing these flavors and then season afterward where appropriate—a great ethos to have across the board when making soups.

A heads-up: A few of the recipes use particular seafood and Chinese sour mustard greens (*suan cai*), which are not always easily accessible to everyone, so plan in advance where possible. I've put a few helpful hints in the recipes for substitutes so everyone can give each meal a shot; the rest of the ingredients are otherwise easy to find.

PORK AND PICKLED GREENS NOODLE SOUP

Sour mustard greens (suan cai) are the quintessential element of this dish—and the quintessential element in a northern Chinese pantry. This one ingredient can give so much complexity without the need for many other items. For first-timers, sour mustard greens should be easily bought from your local Asian grocer.

Here, the mustard greens give this dish a slightly sour and tangy edge that refreshes the umami pork broth. I use pork bones when I make this broth—the sweetest meat is closest to the bone. Once you've cooked them down for hours and made your flavorsome broth, shred all the meat off the bone and chuck it back into the mixture.

SERVES 4

Soup Base

1¾ lb (800 g) pork chuck bones

2 tbsp (50 g) sliced fresh ginger

2 spring onions, white part only

1½ tsp (3 g) dried shrimps, rinsed

2 tbsp (30 ml) Shaoxing rice wine

8½ cups (2 L) water

4 tbsp (60 ml) light soy sauce

4 tsp (20 g) rock sugar

Salt

14 oz (400 g) pickled mustard greens, rinsed, sliced into 2" (5-cm) pieces

17 oz (480 g) thin-cut Egg Noodles (page 157)

Spring onion, for serving

Fresh cilantro, for serving

Make the soup base: In a large pot over high heat, combine the pork chuck bones, ginger, spring onion white parts, dried shrimps, Shaoxing wine and water. Bring to a boil, then lower the heat and simmer for 90 minutes, or until the meat is falling off the bone. Remove from the heat and let cool. Remove the ginger and spring onion pieces and scoop the pork chuck bones into a bowl. Using your hands, shred all the meat off the bones and place the shreds back into the pot of soup. Season with the light soy sauce, rock sugar and salt to taste. Increase the heat to high and bring back to a boil, then add the pickled mustard greens. Cook for 3 minutes and taste, seasoning as required. It should have a balance of sweet, savory, salty and sour flavors.

Bring a separate large pot of water to a boil, then cook the noodles for about 3 minutes, or until just cooked through. Drain, then divide among four serving bowls followed by a generous ladle of the soup. Top with spring onion and cilantro before serving.

VIETNAMESE CRAB BROTH WITH THICK RICE NOODLES

The shell of the crab is important for infusing the flavor into a dish, so if you like a rich broth it is certainly worth sourcing fresh crabs. Crabmeat works amazingly, too, for the Vietnamese crab broth (*bún riêu*). Using the crabmeat and a few other meat and seafood components, we are binding all the proteins together to make a combination meatball to sit in this punchy and flavor-packed Vietnamese soup, with some thick rice noodles to slurp it down with.

SERVES 4

Soup

2¼ lb (1 kg) pork spareribs, cut into 2" (5-cm) pieces

1 tbsp (5 g) dried shrimps, rinsed

1 tsp salt

8½ cups (2 L) water

3 tbsp (45 ml) vegetable oil

3 spring onions, finely chopped

1 tsp chili powder

6 tomatoes, halved

2 cups + 2 tbsp (500 ml) chicken stock

3 tbsp (45 ml) Asian fish sauce, plus more to taste

2 blue swimmer crabs, cleaned and halved

Make the soup: In a large pot over high heat, combine the pork spareribs, dried shrimps, salt and water. Bring to a boil, then lower the heat and simmer for 1 hour, or until the meat is tender. While the soup is cooking, in a small skillet over medium heat, heat the vegetable oil, then add the spring onions and chili powder. Cook for 2 to 3 minutes, then remove from the heat. Add this to the pork soup along with the tomatoes, chicken stock, fish sauce and the two blue swimmer crabs. Simmer for another 20 minutes.

(continued)

CLASSIC PORK WONTON NOODLE SOUP

A good broth is the foundation for so many good dishes, but what makes a good broth? In my opinion, a neutral broth (meat only) is best. Some cuisines tend to use a mirepoix (a mixture of diced onion, carrot and celery) for their broth bases, but in most cases, less is more. Keeping it simple means that your broth starts off at a versatile base level from which you can go in any direction you want and season or modify your noodle soup to your liking, but in any good takeout-style wonton noodle soup, the beauty is in the simplicity.

I'm using my Mum's Crispy Pork Wontons (page 136) in this dish, but substituting frozen wontons will still be a passing grade. I eat mine with a gooey Marbled Tea Egg (page 127), so that yolk gets into the broth, too, for some added richness.

SERVES 4

Pork Bone Broth

1¾ lb (800 g) pork chuck bones

7 tbsp (40 g) sliced fresh ginger

1 spring onion, white part only

1 tsp dried shrimps, rinsed

2 tbsp (30 ml) Shaoxing rice wine

8½ cups (2 L) water

Salt

Pork Wonton Filling

7 oz (200 g) fatty ground pork

6 tbsp (30 g) grated fresh ginger

1 tbsp (15 ml) oyster sauce

1 tsp sesame oil

1 tsp cornstarch

Pinch of freshly ground white pepper

Pinch of salt

20 wonton wrappers

Scant 3 oz (80 g) thin-cut Egg Noodles (page 157)

Bunch of bok choy, trimmed

Sliced spring onion, for garnish

Fried garlic flakes, for garnish

Make the pork bone broth: In a large pot over high heat, combine the pork chuck bones, ginger, spring onion, dried shrimps, Shaoxing wine and water. Bring to a boil, then lower the heat and simmer for 90 minutes. Remove from the heat and strain the liquid into another pot. Season with salt as required.

Make the wonton filling: In a medium-sized bowl, combine all the filling ingredients and mix vigorously in one direction until the mixture binds. Cover and leave to rest in the fridge for 30 minutes.

To assemble, place one wonton wrapper on a clean surface. Place a heaping teaspoon of the mixture in the center and brush half of the edges of the wrapper with water. Fold the wet edges over (in half) to make a rectangular shape and enclose the filling. Brush one of the corners with water and fold inward to overlap with the other corner. Press to seal and transfer to a baking sheet lined with parchment paper. Continue until all the remaining wontons are formed.

Bring a large pot of water to a boil, then cook the noodles for about 3 minutes, or until just cooked through. Remove them from the pot, using a mesh strainer, drain and divide among four serving bowls. Cook the wontons in the same boiling water until cooked through, 4 to 6 minutes. Remove from the water, using a slotted spoon, and divide among the serving bowls. Blanch the bok choy in the boiling water until just cooked, about 1 minute. Remove with a slotted spoon and divide among the serving bowls. Ladle the pork bone broth over the wontons, noodles and bok choy and top with spring onion and fried garlic flakes. Serve immediately.

BRAISED OXTAIL NOODLE SOUP

Oxtail might seem like a strange thing to eat, but like most lesser-quality cuts of meat, it lends itself beautifully to being broken down in a soup. Most recipes call for roasting the oxtails first, then dropping them into the pot once caramelized. To save on time (even more), you can skip this step and drop them straight into your empty pot or pressure cooker, brown them off a bit in there and add your water.

Similar to the Lanzhou Beef Hand-Pulled Noodles (page 12) but with fewer ingredients—this soup is all about making the oxtail the hero, with a solid soy base and some subtle undertones of spice.

SERVES 4

Broth

2¼ lb (1 kg) beef oxtails

8½ cups (2 L) water

1 onion, halved

7 tbsp (40 g) peeled and sliced fresh ginger

2 star anise

1 piece dried orange peel

1 tsp black peppercorns

2 tbsp (30 ml) dark soy sauce

Salt

1 daikon radish, peeled and cut into ¾" (2-cm) rounds

17 oz (480 g) thin-cut Hand-Cut Wheat Noodles (page 155)

Roughly chopped fresh cilantro, for serving

Make the broth: Preheat the oven to 400°F (200°C). Place the oxtails on a baking sheet lined with parchment paper and roast in the oven for 45 minutes, turning halfway through. Once they've roasted, fill a large pot over medium heat with the water. Add the roasted oxtails, onion, ginger, star anise, dried orange peel, black peppercorns and dark soy sauce. Bring to a boil, then lower the heat to a simmer. Cover and let cook very gently for 3 to 4 hours.

To finish the broth, carefully remove the oxtails from the pot and transfer to a bowl. Strain the soup and return to the pot over low heat. Season with salt to taste and add the daikon. Let cook for another 30 minutes, or until the radish has softened. Hand-shred the meat from the oxtail when it is cool enough to handle and add to the soup.

Bring a large pot of water to a boil, then cook the noodles for about 3 minutes, or until just cooked through. Drain, then divide among four serving bowls. Ladle on the hot broth with its shredded oxtail and daikon. Garnish with cilantro before serving.

CROSSING-THE-BRIDGE NOODLE SOUP

Crossing-the-bridge noodles (*guo qiao mi xian*) is one of the great signature dishes of the Yunnan province in China, and is aptly named after the story of a scholar studying for his imperial exams, whose wife would cross a bridge to bring him noodles, but the noodles would get cold by the time she got there. She created a method of pouring a layer of oil on top of the broth to keep it hot enough. Her scholar-husband passed his exam and the rest, as they say, is history. Although Yunnan food is predominantly sour, that takes the backseat in this dish and really brings harmony to the delicate flavors of the soup. This recipe has a few elements—a delicately spiced broth, a dipping sauce, toppings and some thin rice noodles—but to do it justice, none can be compromised on. Go hard on the toppings!

SERVES 4

Chicken Broth

8½ cups (2 L) water

2 chicken carcasses

4 slices fresh ginger

2 spring onions, white part only

2 cloves garlic

1 tsp Sichuan peppercorns (optional)

1 tbsp (15 ml) Shaoxing rice wine

2 tbsp (30 ml) light soy sauce

Salt

To Serve

7 oz (200 g) pickled mustard greens, rinsed and roughly chopped

Bunch of bok choy, thinly sliced

1 (14-oz [400-g]) can quail eggs, drained

3.5 oz (100 g) skinless chicken breast, sliced paper thin

3.5 g (100 g) pork tenderloin, sliced paper thin

1 lb (450 g) Thin Rice Noodles (page 159), freshly cooked

Roughly chopped fresh cilantro

The OG Chili Sauce (page 148)

Make the chicken broth: Fill a large pot over medium heat with the water. Add the chicken carcasses, ginger, spring onion white parts, garlic, Sichuan peppercorns (if using) and Shaoxing wine. Bring to a boil, then lower the heat to a simmer. Cover and let cook very gently for 2 hours, stirring every 30 minutes.

To finish the chicken broth, strain into a large bowl to remove all the aromatics and bones. Return the liquid to the pot and leave over low heat. Add the light soy sauce and salt to taste.

To serve, divide the mustard greens, bok choy, quail eggs, a few slices of chicken and pork among four serving bowls. Increase the heat under the soup to high and wait until it boils. Carefully ladle the boiling hot soup into your serving bowls to cook the chicken and pork. Add the cooked rice noodles and garnish with cilantro. Serve with the OG chili sauce on the side for dipping.

SIX

"THESE AREN'T NOODLES!"

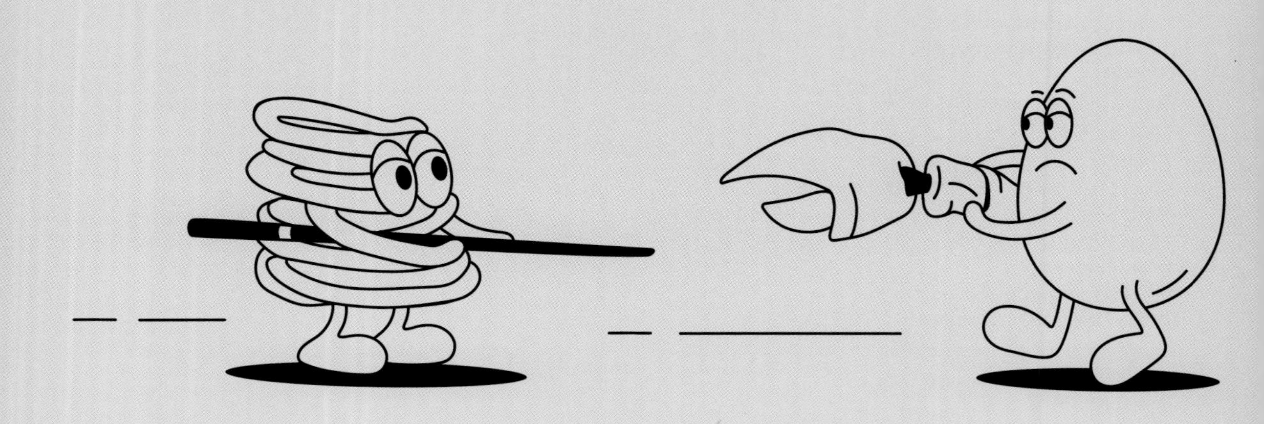

Isn't it interesting that someone back in the day discovered that mixing grain and water makes dough, then it traveled to many cultures before evolving into what we have today? This chapter is a bit of an ode to some of those more unconventional forms of noodles, so different in form to the modern commercial ones, that it raises the question: Are these noodles?

Back to basics: A dough can be made from many different grains and starches, and into noodles of many different morphologies. This same logic is what allows all the different varieties of pasta to be called pasta. Risoni, cavatelli, pappardelle, cannelloni—all are so different in shape, but all can be made from the same base dough. So, why shouldn't it be the same for noodles?

The form of each noodle variation in this chapter is linked to its functionality, reflecting the sauce it goes well with, whether it should be filled (or not), or features of the dish that the noodle is trying to highlight or balance out. Perhaps the most relevant example of this is the Cat's Ear Noodles with XO (page 98). You might recognize that these "non-noodles" are similar in structure to the pasta shape called conchiglie, named for its shell shape. Conchiglie is also similar in function to the cat's ear noodles, in that serves as a vessel to scoop up the sauce it's paired with. Form reflects function.

The first recipe—Spicy Cold Skin Noodles (page 91)—takes the concept of "Are these noodles?" to the next level, by making a wheat dough and then deconstructing it to produce two very different components that form the integral parts of the dish. And that's what this chapter is all about—challenging what a noodle really is, exploration and having some fun!

HOT OIL SCISSOR-CUT NOODLES

Dāoxiāomiàn, or sliced noodles, are a humble hand-cut noodle variant, but not how you think (and possibly not how you're used to). To me, a hand-cut noodle is one that is a bit rustic and doesn't use a machine, whereas these noodles are shaved from a block of dough, using a knife, into a pot of boiling water, producing wide strips of noodles. To be on the safe side, I find a pair of scissors makes a great and much safer alternative to a knife—and to the same effect—so that's what I've done for my version of dāoxiāomiàn.

SERVES 2 OR 3

---

1 lb (450 g) Hand-Cut Wheat Noodle dough (page 155)

2 tbsp (12 g) chopped spring onion

3 cloves garlic, finely minced

2 tbsp (7 g) Chinese chili flakes

Salt

½ cup (120 ml) vegetable oil

2 tbsp (30 ml) light soy sauce

1 tbsp (15 ml) dark soy sauce

1 tbsp (15 ml) Chinese black vinegar

To Serve

Chopped fresh cilantro

Sliced spring onion

Toasted white sesame seeds

Make the noodles: Bring a large pot of water to a boil. Form the dough into a ball and hold it over the pot with your nondominant hand. With your dominant hand, cut off little bits of dough with kitchen scissors so that they drop into the water. The cut parts of dough will form curled strips. Let cook for 4 to 5 minutes, or until the noodles float to the top. Drain and divide among two or three serving bowls.

In the center of the bowl, on top of the noodles, carefully arrange the spring onion, garlic, chili flakes and salt in a mound. In a small pot, heat the vegetable oil until smoking and carefully pour it over the spring onion mixture. It should sizzle on contact. Add the light soy sauce, dark soy sauce and Chinese black vinegar equally to each bowl, and toss to combine. Top with cilantro, spring onion and sesame seeds. Serve immediately.

CAT'S EAR NOODLES WITH XO

This "non-noodle" features flat pieces of dough, around 1 inch (2.5 cm) long, that curl inward slightly upon cooking, resembling the ears of a cat. While they may not look like traditional noodles, they certainly come from a noodle dough, and by now we should know that noodles can come in many shapes, sizes and textures.

The divot that forms in the center of the "ear" is perfect for scooping up the hot bean sauce that goes with it as intended. Don't be too concerned with the shape consistency—real cats' ears come in all sorts, too!

SERVES 4

1 lb (450 g) Hand-Cut Wheat Noodle dough (page 155)

Cornstarch, for dusting

Generous 5.5 oz (160 g) Vegan XO Sauce (page 151), for serving

Mung bean sprouts, for serving

Fresh cilantro, for serving

Divide the dough into four equal portions. Keep covered with a clean, lightly damp tea towel, to prevent from drying out. Working with one portion at a time, roll it into a long log about the thickness of your finger. Dust with cornstarch if it is too wet or sticky. Using a pastry scraper or butter knife, cut the log into pieces about ⅜ inch (1 cm) long. Working with one small piece of dough at a time, use your thumb to gently push into the dough and away from you. The dough will form a concave shape, like an ear, against your thumb. Repeat this process with the remaining dough. Dust with more cornstarch to prevent the ear noodles from sticking and space them out as you work so they aren't touching.

Bring a large pot of water to a boil, then cook the noodles for about 3 minutes. Drain and divide among four serving bowls. Top with a generous amount of vegan XO sauce and toss gently. Garnish with mung bean sprouts and cilantro before serving.

COLD CHINESE JELLY NOODLES (LIANGFEN)

Like the Spicy Cold Skin Noodles (page 91), this signature Sichuan dish is full of spicy, tongue-numbing flavor. *Liang* means "cold" in Mandarin, and this cold noodle element offers some reprieve from the intense building heat from the sauce. The jelly noodles, made from mung bean starch, turn a ghostly white upon cooking and have a slightly bouncy texture—like jelly!

SERVES 4

Jelly Noodles

1 cup (58 g) mung bean starch

1 cup + 2 tsp (250 ml) water, at room temperature

3¾ cups (875 ml) boiling water

Chunky Noodle Salsa (page 152)

¼ cup (35 g) chopped roasted peanuts, for serving

Thinly sliced spring onion, for serving

Make the jelly noodles: In a medium-sized bowl, combine the mung bean starch with the cup plus 2 tablespoons (250 ml) of room-temperature water and stir well. Fill a medium-sized pot with the 3¾ cups (875 ml) of boiling water and place over medium heat. Once again at a boil, lower the heat and whisk constantly while slowly pouring the starch mixture into the pot. Continuing to whisk, cook for 5 to 6 minutes. The mixture will thicken and become translucent. Carefully pour into a rectangular 8-inch (20-cm)-long baking dish and let sit at room temperature for about 2 hours. Once the jelly has formed, slice into noodle strands a little thicker than udon noodles.

To serve, divide the cold jelly noodles among four serving bowls. Add a generous amount of chunky noodle salsa, about ¼ cup (65 g) per serving, and toss gently. Top with the roasted peanuts and spring onion before serving.

LOBSTER FRIED NOODLE BASKET

Fried noodle baskets are often delicious if done right. There are both wet and dry noodles in this dish, as some of the noodles get deep-fried into the shape of a bowl, serving as the vessel for the rich lobster stir-fry. Similar to the Chicken Khao Soi Noodles (page 39), textural contrast is very important for this recipe. This dish grants you a textural odyssey as you make your way through the course—wet saucy noodles with delicate lobster flesh, the slightly moistened stodgy fried noodles on the inner bowl wall and the super-crunchy noodles on the outer wall. Hot tip: Eat your way from the outside of the bowl inward, or you might find yourself eating off the table!

SERVES 2

10.5 oz (300 g) thin-cut Egg Noodles (page 157)

2 tbsp (16 g) cornstarch

Lobster Stir-Fry

2¼ lb (1 kg) lobster tail

Vegetable oil, to fill fryer plus 2 tbsp (30 ml) for cooking

2 spring onions, cut into 2" (5-cm) pieces

8 thin slices fresh ginger

1 tbsp (8 g) cornstarch + 2 tbsp (30 ml) water

Stir-Fry Sauce

2 tbsp (30 ml) oyster sauce

1 tbsp (15 ml) light soy sauce

1 tbsp (15 ml) Shaoxing rice wine

1 tsp superfine sugar

½ tsp sesame oil

Salt

Pinch of freshly ground white pepper

½ cup + 2 tbsp (150 ml) chicken stock

Sliced spring onion, for garnish

Bring a large pot of water to a boil, then cook the noodles for about 3 minutes. Drain and set aside about half of the noodles. Transfer the remaining noodles to a bowl and add the cornstarch. Toss until well combined. Press the noodles firmly into a large metal sieve to form a basket, then set aside.

Start the lobster stir-fry: Slice the lobster tail in half lengthwise and chop into 2-inch (5-cm) pieces. Rinse gently to clean, then pat dry. Fill a wok with vegetable oil and heat to 350°F (180°C). Test by dipping a wooden chopstick into the oil: The chopstick will sizzle when the oil is ready. Gently lower the lobster pieces into the oil and flash fry for about 30 seconds to seal all juices inside. Remove the lobster pieces, drain on a plate lined with paper towels and set aside. Gently lower the metal sieve holding the noodles into the wok to fry until golden brown and crispy, 4 to 5 minutes. Drain on a separate plate lined with paper towels.

Make the stir-fry sauce: In a small bowl, combine all the sauce ingredients and mix well. Set aside until required.

To complete the stir-fry, place the wok over medium to high heat. Heat the vegetable oil, then add the spring onions and ginger. Stir-fry for 1 to 2 minutes, or until fragrant, then add the stir-fry sauce. Bring to a boil, add the fried lobster and reserved cooked noodles, and cook for another 2 minutes, tossing gently to incorporate the sauce. In a small bowl, stir together the cornstarch and water to make a slurry. Stir in the slurry to thicken the sauce, then cook for another 2 minutes.

To serve, turn your noodle basket the right side up on a serving dish. Pour in the lobster stir-fry into the center of the basket and garnish with spring onion. Serve immediately.

SHEET NOODLE CHICKEN SOUP

One of my family's traditional dishes is a very simple meat bone broth with winter melon. If you haven't had it before, winter melon is a very neutral ingredient and really serves to take on the soup's flavor while adding a fleshy crunch. We don't normally have it with noodles, but I've added them because I absolutely love thick-cut noodles: They're such generous pieces of noodles that can also carry so much of the soup's flavor, plus they're more fun to eat!

For this recipe, I've cut wheat dough into broad, long, rectangular sheets. Although not quite lasagna sheets, the comparably bigger size of these noodles means it takes less time to make them. Simple chicken soup with winter melon and some super-thick noodles—get ready to take it wide!

SERVES 4

Chicken Soup

6⅓ cups (1.5 L) chicken stock

2 slices fresh ginger

17.5 oz (500 g) chicken thighs, cut into 1¼" (3-cm) pieces

1 tbsp (15 ml) Shaoxing rice wine

17.5 oz (500 g) winter melon, peeled, seeded and cut into 1¼" (3-cm) pieces

1 tomato, cut into 8 pieces

2 tbsp (30 ml) light soy sauce

Salt

1 lb (450 g) Hand-Cut Wheat Noodle dough (page 155)

Cornstarch, for dusting

Sliced spring onion, for serving

Make the chicken soup: Place a large pot filled with the chicken stock over medium heat. Add the ginger, chicken thigh pieces and Shaoxing wine, and let simmer for 30 minutes. Add the winter melon and tomato, and let simmer for another 20 minutes. Add the light soy sauce and salt to taste. Keep warm until required.

Make the sheet noodles: Form the dough into two equal portions. Lightly dust your counter with cornstarch and roll one portion of dough into a long rectangular sheet about 1⁄16 inch (2 mm) thick. Cut it into 1½-inch (4-cm)-wide sheets. Bring a large pot of water to a boil, then cook the noodles for about 3 minutes. Drain and transfer to the chicken soup. Serve immediately, garnished with the spring onion.

SEVEN

NOODLES WITH A TWIST

Unapologetically, this chapter is about fusing cooking techniques from different cultures to create tasty and unique dishes. I've taken inspiration from a range of gastronomical styles and cultures—Italian, Thai, Japanese . . . and maintained some Chinese influences, too. These new recipes are certainly not defined or contained by cultural tradition, but have been developed to marry complementary flavors, textures and journeys.

The best thing about "breaking from tradition" in cooking, and especially with fusion cuisine, is that you can take what you love about one cuisine or dish, and marry it with something else you love from another! You can "borrow" almost any style of cooking and apply it to a noodle—I've even seen deep-fried noodle balls! Or blend "traditional" ingredients or sauces . . . the opportunities for cross-pollination of styles, ingredients and ideas are limitless, really. In many cases, certainly not all, the offspring of the union is actually something worthwhile—cooking and eating.

The first two recipes are fusion twists on pasta classics or fusion twists on Asian classics, depending on how you see it!

SUPER-SPEEDY GARLIC NOODLES

I'm a sucker for two things; cheesy garlicky pasta and thin-cut egg noodles—so what better way to enjoy them both than to literally enjoy them together? Although cheese doesn't get featured often in Chinese cuisine, pecorino is—in essence—a super-salty element, like soy. Garlic, spring onion and chives are all kindred spirits, used in both Italian and Chinese cooking despite their having quite different flavor profiles. Any ingredient, used in the right way, can potentially lend itself beautifully to a fusion of cuisines. Thin egg noodles that meld Italian and Chinese cuisine turn out to be a delightfully delectable, savory snack.

SERVES 2

---

12 oz (340) g thin-cut Egg Noodles (page 157)

3 tbsp (42 g) unsalted butter

2 tbsp (30 ml) olive oil

8 cloves garlic, peeled

2 spring onions, sliced

4 tsp (20 ml) oyster sauce

4 tsp (20 ml) light soy sauce

1½ tsp (8 g) light brown sugar

Dash of sesame oil

¼ cup (25 g) pecorino cheese

Salt

2 tbsp (6 g) finely chopped fresh chives

Bring a large pot of water to a boil, then cook the noodles for about 3 minutes. Drain the noodles and reserve 1 to 2 tablespoons (15 to 30 ml) of the cooking water.

In a large skillet over medium heat, heat the unsalted butter and olive oil. Once the butter has melted, lower the heat to as low as you can and add the garlic and spring onions. Cook for 6 to 8 minutes, or until fragrant, being careful not to let the garlic brown. Meanwhile, in a small bowl, combine the oyster sauce, light soy sauce, brown sugar and sesame oil, and whisk until they just come together. Increase the heat, add your cooked noodles, the sauce that was just mixed up and the pecorino cheese. Toss gently until well incorporated and season with salt, if required. If the sauce is a little thick, add the reserved cooking liquid and toss. Transfer to a serving platter and top with the chives before serving.

CACIO E PEPE UDON NOODLES

Cacio e pepe is all about the cheese and pepper and is usually served with spaghetti pasta. Borrowing from the concept of the Super-Speedy Garlic Noodles (page 109), I've pumped up this very core Italian dish with some Japanese staples. Miso and *furikake* seasoning (toasted sesame, nori, salt and sugar) give these noodles an umami, briny hit. I've traded out the thin spaghetti for some thick and chewy udon to add that additional bouncy texture to harmonize with the cheese.

To get the udon thick and juicy—just how I like it—I'd recommend using a bread flour. Bread flour is higher in gluten and protein than all-purpose flour, which gives the dough more gluten, more stretch; and the udon, their iconic texture.

SERVES 4

17.5 oz (480 g) thick-cut udon-style Hand-Cut Wheat Noodles (page 155)

2 tbsp (32 g) white miso paste

Scant 6 tbsp (80 g) unsalted butter, cut into cubes

1 tbsp (6 g) freshly ground black pepper, plus more for serving

Generous 2 oz (60 g) Parmesan cheese, finely grated, plus more for serving

Pinch of salt

Finely sliced spring onion, for serving

Furikake, for serving

Bring a large pot of water to a boil, then cook the noodles for about 3 minutes. Drain the noodles and reserve ¾ cup plus 2 teaspoons (200 ml) of the cooking water. Whisk the miso into the reserved cooking water until well incorporated and set aside. Set the noodles aside, too.

Place a pan over medium heat and add half the butter. Once the butter has melted, add the black pepper and cook for about 30 seconds, or until fragrant. Add half of the miso liquid, noodles and the remaining butter. Add the Parmesan and season with a pinch of salt.

Toss the noodles in the pan until well coated, creamy and the cheese has melted. Add a little more of the miso liquid if it is too dry and continue to toss. Transfer to a serving platter and top with extra pepper, Parmesan, spring onion and furikake.

SQUID NOODLE PAD THAI

Another recipe I've been lucky enough to discover while exploring some noodle variations is my twist on the traditional pad thai. However, it wouldn't be a pad thai without its signature sweet tamarind sauce so I've kept that characteristic in this dish. But I've also made some core tweaks—squid tubes thinly sliced into long strips serve as the noodles in the dish! If you're cooking squid for the first time, make sure to cook it very gently over low heat, so it doesn't go tough. Raw squid is slightly opaque in appearance, but goes a solid white once cooked, so look out for the color change and remove it from the pan as soon as it happens.

SERVES 2

---

14 oz (400 g) squid tubes

Scant 3 tbsp (40 g) clarified butter

Pinch of salt

Pinch of freshly ground white pepper

Pad Thai Sauce

5 tsp (25 ml) tamarind puree

2 tbsp (30 g) light brown sugar

2 tbsp (30 ml) Asian fish sauce

5 tsp (25 ml) oyster sauce

To Stir-Fry

2 tbsp (30 ml) vegetable oil

1 clove garlic, finely chopped

½ white onion, sliced

5.5 oz (150 g) pork loin, thinly sliced

2 large eggs, lightly whisked

1 cup (100 g) mung bean sprouts

¼ cup (13 g) garlic chives, cut into 1" (2.5-cm) pieces

¼ cup (35 g) finely chopped peanuts

To Serve

Finely chopped peanuts

Mung bean sprouts

Red pepper flakes (optional)

Lime wedges

Clean the squid well under running water, then pat dry. Slice the squid tubes lengthwise into long, noodlelike strips and set aside, refrigerated, until required.

Make the pad thai sauce: In a small bowl, combine all the sauce ingredients and mix well. Set aside until required.

In a large skillet over medium heat, heat the clarified butter. Once hot, add the squid and season with salt and pepper. Cook for 2 to 3 minutes, or until just cooked through and opaque. Remove from the heat and set aside.

Start the stir-fry: In a wok over high heat, heat the vegetable oil. Once hot, add the garlic and onion, and cook for 1 to 2 minutes. Add the sliced pork and cook for another 2 minutes, stirring until the pork is cooked through. Remove the pork and set aside, add the whisked eggs to the wok and cook, stirring, until scrambled. Add back the pork along with the mung bean sprouts, squid noodles and pad thai sauce. Toss gently and cook for another 2 minutes. Add the garlic chives and peanuts, and toss before removing from the heat. Transfer to a serving platter and sprinkle with additional peanuts, bean sprouts and a sprinkle of red pepper flakes, if desired. Squeeze lime juice over all before eating.

ASIAN GREEN PESTO NOODLES

Keeping on the fusion train, these tasty green miso noodles get their vibrant color and taste from an Asian-style green sauce. Instead of the basil and Parmesan (like in your traditional pesto Genovese), I've used Chinese broccoli leaves, cilantro and miso to create all the characteristics of a pesto, but with an Asian palate.

Get your blender ready. Once you've blitzed up your green sauce, boil your noodles, toss them through with some butter and mix with your pesto.

SERVES 4

Asian Green Pesto

2 cups (140 g) Chinese broccoli leaves

2 cups (35 g) cilantro leaves

2 tbsp (30 ml) fresh orange juice

1 tbsp (15 ml) fresh lemon juice

1 tbsp (15 ml) rice vinegar

1½ tbsp (24 g) white miso paste

1 clove garlic

½ cup + 1 tsp (125 ml) vegetable oil

1 tsp toasted sesame oil

¼ tsp freshly ground white pepper

Salt

1 lb (450 g) thin-cut Hand-Cut Wheat Noodles (page 155)

Toasted white sesame seeds, for serving

2 spring onions, thinly sliced, for serving

Make the pesto: In a blender, combine all the pesto ingredients, except the salt, and blitz until smooth and creamy. If not green enough, add a little more Chinese broccoli leaves and blitz again. Season with salt to taste and set aside.

Bring a large pot of water to a boil, then cook the noodles for about 3 minutes. Drain and toss with the Asian green pesto until well coated. Transfer to your serving bowls and top with toasted sesame seeds and spring onion before serving.

TOFU AND BLACK FUNGUS NOODLE SALAD

This is a fresh vegan noodle salad, dressed with my favorite duo—black vinegar and Chinese chili oil. For added texture and freshness, I slice the *wombok* (napa cabbage) and the tofu sheets into long, thin strips, comparable in width and length to the soba noodles. This means they mix with the noodles easily, but also provide a combination of textures and visually resemble a bit of an optical illusion. I'd recommend slicing the black fungus thinly, too—unless you are using fresh, rehydrated dried black fungus can be a bit on the tough side.

FYI: There are two types of tofu skin sheets, and for this recipe we want the thinly pressed tofu skin sheets, not the dried bean curd skin (*yuba*). Both of these will be stocked at any good Asian grocer, but the one we want will be in the fridge section with the other cold tofu products.

SERVES 4

Salad

3.5 oz (100 g) thin-sheet tofu, sliced into long strips resembling noodles

Generous 1 oz (30 g) dried black fungus

14 oz (400 g) Buckwheat (Soba) Noodles (page 162)

1 carrot, peeled, cut into thin matchsticks

1 cucumber, thinly sliced into ribbons

¼ cup (5 g) fresh cilantro, roughly chopped

¼ cup (10 g) fresh mint leaves

¼ cup (10 g) fresh Thai basil leaves

4 spring onions, thinly sliced

½ cup (46 g) finely shredded wombok

2 tsp (6 g) toasted white sesame seeds

Black vinegar dressing (page 92)

Chinese Chili Oil (page 147), for serving

Place a medium-sized pot of water over medium to high heat. Once boiling, add the tofu strips and stir briefly. Drain, rinse under cold water and set aside in the fridge to cool. Next, soak the black fungus in hot water for about 30 minutes, or until softened. Drain and slice into long, thin strips.

Bring a large pot of water to a boil, then cook the noodles for about 1 minute. Drain and rinse with cold water. Place the noodles in a large bowl along with the tofu, black fungus, carrot, cucumber, cilantro, mint, Thai basil, spring onions, wombok and toasted white sesame seeds. Pour the black vinegar dressing over all and toss gently until well incorporated. Transfer to four serving bowls and drizzle with Chinese chili oil.

NOTE:

- Fresh pressed tofu skin sheets can be found at most Asian grocers.

INSTANT TOMATO EGG DROP NOODLE SOUP

Egg drop soup is entrenched in Chinese cuisine and universal to most neighborhood Chinese restaurants. There are many variations, but all have in common the "dropping," or slow trickling of beaten egg into a hot broth, creating ribbons of silky egg streaming throughout. My modest variation is vegetarian and uses a spring onion and ginger base, tomatoes (fresh or canned) and vegetable stock, served with some egg noodles. Once your soup is developed, get a whirlpool going and slowly trickle in your beaten eggs.

SERVES 2

Scant 9 oz (250 g) thin-cut Egg Noodles (page 157)

3 tbsp (45 ml) vegetable oil, plus more as needed

2 cloves garlic, minced

½ tsp minced fresh ginger

2 spring onions, thinly sliced, white and green part separated

2 to 3 large tomatoes, chopped

5½ cups (1.3 L) vegetable stock

2 tbsp (30 ml) light soy sauce

½ tsp sesame oil

1 tsp superfine sugar

Salt

Pinch of freshly ground white pepper

2 large eggs

Bring a large pot of water to a boil, then cook the noodles for about 3 minutes. Drain, toss with a little oil to prevent sticking and divide between two serving bowls.

In a small pot over medium heat, heat the vegetable oil. When hot, add the garlic, ginger and the white part of the spring onions. Cook for 1 minute, or until softened, then add the tomatoes. Cook for about 5 minutes, stirring, until the tomato starts to soften. Add the vegetable stock, light soy sauce, sesame oil, superfine sugar, salt to taste and white pepper. Stir well, then cover and simmer for 5 minutes.

Crack the eggs into a small bowl and whisk. Uncover the pot and increase the heat to medium. Stir the soup constantly while slowly pouring in the beaten eggs. Pour over the noodles and garnish the green part of the spring onions. Serve immediately.

VEGAN SHIITAKE DAN DAN NOODLES

These vegan Dan Dan noodles are taken straight off the Bumplings menu. Every week at Bumplings, we sell hundreds of Dan Dan noodles, and with meat reductionism on the rise, I make it one of my goals to have tasty alternatives for non-meat-eaters.

Ground pork is a more passive element in the conventional form of this noodle dish, so it's not a deal breaker to opt for a vegan alternative. Plus, the chili oil, spices and sour mustard greens are the major players in classic Dan Dan noodles, so it's easy to swap out the meat for some finely chopped vegetables or mushrooms.

SERVES 4

Mushroom Mixture

2 tbsp (30 ml) vegetable oil

7 oz (200 g) rehydrated dried shiitake mushrooms, minced

2 tsp (10 ml) hoisin sauce

2 tsp (10 ml) Shaoxing rice wine

1 tsp dark soy sauce

3.5 oz (50 g) pickled mustard greens

Dan Dan Sauce

2 tbsp (30 g) tahini

3 tbsp (45 ml) light soy sauce

2 tbsp (30 ml) Chinese black vinegar

2 tsp (8 g) superfine sugar

½ cup + 1 tsp (125 ml) Chinese Chili Oil (page 147)

1 clove garlic, minced

1 lb (450 g) thin-cut Hand-Cut Wheat Noodles (page 155)

Bunch of choy sum, trimmed, for serving

Chopped roasted peanuts, for serving

Chopped spring onion, for serving

Chinese Chili Oil (page 147), for drizzling

Make the mushroom mixture: In a wok over medium heat, heat the vegetable oil. Add the minced mushrooms and cook, stirring constantly, until cooked through and browned. Add the hoisin, Shaoxing wine and dark soy sauce. Cook, stirring, until the liquid has evaporated. Add the pickled mustard greens and cook for another 3 minutes. Remove from the heat and transfer to a bowl. Set aside until required.

Make the sauce: In a bowl, combine all the sauce ingredients and stir well. Loosen with a little hot water, if required.

Bring a large pot of salted water to a boil, then cook the noodles for 2 to 3 minutes, or until they rise to the surface. Blanch the choy sum separately and drain.

To serve, divide the Dan Dan sauce among four bowls, followed by the noodles, choy sum, cooked mushroom mixture, chopped peanuts and spring onion. Drizzle with Chinese chili oil and serve immediately.

MAURITIAN FAMILY FRIED NOODLES

Another staple in my family comes from the blending of two cuisines from China and Mauritius, and stems from a preference for authentic, unpretentiously delicious food! It's similar to a Chinese fried rice and has all the elements you'd expect: *lap cheong* (Chinese sausage), omelet, prawns and chicken. I prefer to use chicken thigh as they stay moist and the fat gets rendered off, joining the sauce for full flavor. These noodles are oyster sauce–heavy, but with all the usual suspects in there, too.

SERVES 4 TO 6

Marinated Chicken

3 boneless, skinless chicken thighs, cut into ¾" (2-cm) strips

½ tsp freshly ground black pepper

1 tbsp (15 ml) light soy sauce

1 tbsp (15 ml) Shaoxing rice wine

1 tsp cornstarch

1 tsp sesame oil

Fried Noodles

3 tbsp (45 ml) vegetable oil, divided, for wok

5.5 oz (150 g) prawns, peeled and deveined

Salt and freshly ground black pepper

3 large eggs, whisked

⅔ cup (60 g) shredded Chinese cabbage

⅔ cup (90 g) matchstick-cut carrot

3 spring onions, white part sliced, green part cut into 1½" (4-cm) lengths

2¼ lb (1 kg) Hokkien noodles or wide egg noodles (store-bought)

2 Chinese sausages, microwaved with a little water, then sliced

2 tbsp (30 ml) light soy sauce

2 tbsp (30 ml) oyster sauce

1 cup (100 g) mung bean sprouts

To Serve

The OG Chili Sauce (page 148)

Prepare the marinated chicken mixture: In a medium-sized bowl, mix together all its ingredients. Cover and set aside to marinate for at least 30 minutes.

Make the noodles: In a wok, heat 1 tablespoon (15 ml) of the vegetable oil until hot and fry the prawns, about 3 minutes. Season with a little salt and pepper, remove and set aside.

Keeping the wok over the heat and add another tablespoon (15 ml) of oil. Add the whisked eggs and swirl around the wok to cover as much surface area as possible. After 2 minutes, flip the omelet and cook for another 2 minutes. Slide onto a chopping board and slice into ¾-inch (2-cm) shreds.

Heat the wok until very hot and add the final tablespoon (15 ml) of oil to cook the chicken mixture. Add the marinated chicken and cook until it starts to brown, 4 to 5 minutes. Add the Chinese cabbage, carrot and spring onions, and toss for another 2 to 3 minutes, or until the vegetables are softened.

In a microwave-safe dish, microwave your noodles for about 2 minutes, then add to wok. Toss gently with tongs and continue to cook until the noodles are cooked through, 2 to 3 minutes.

Add the fried prawns, Chinese sausages, light soy sauce and oyster sauce. Adjust for seasoning as desired. Toss and then add the mung bean sprouts before removing from the heat. Serve with the chili sauce.

EIGHT

SLURP N' SNACK

Noodles are great, but sometimes I just want that extra spread of sides to have with my noodles for variety (and for a food coma). Full disclosure: My snacks are usually also some form of carb.

Some of these "noodle snacks" match up with specific recipes quite obviously, such as the Japanese Braised Pork Belly (page 143) with the Braised Pork Shio Ramen (page 20), but others, such as the Marbled Tea Eggs (page 127) are a bit more open to interpretation and your own wants. A boiled egg makes a welcome addition to most noodle soups, in my opinion, and can really be laid in a nest of any kind of noodle.

If I had to choose one to put on a pedestal, the Spring Onion Flower Rolls (page 128) are the dark horse of snacks. They are made using a simple steamed bun dough (I mean, it's basically a noodle . . .) and use a very simple spring onion–rich oil, but they're just so unexpectedly tasty and delicious. This recipe can be good on its own, but if you like carbs with your carbs as I do, it's pretty good with any of the saucy noodle dishes to mop up the juices.

MARBLED TEA EGGS

I love a boiled egg with my noodles. This is a nice food hack to make an impressive side out of some simple boiled eggs. Not only does the marinade give it a nice flavor—that pairs with most Chinese-style noodles—but the overnight soak also means the eggs are easy to shell.

MAKES 8 EGGS

---

8 large eggs, at room temperature

Marinade

2 black tea teabags of your choice

1 bay leaf

1 star anise

1 cinnamon stick

½ tsp Sichuan peppercorns

1 tsp fennel seeds

2 tbsp (30 ml) light soy sauce

2 tbsp (30 ml) dark soy sauce

1 tbsp (15 ml) Shaoxing rice wine

1½ tsp (6 g) superfine sugar

1 tbsp (18 g) salt

Cook the eggs: Place a medium-sized pot filled with lightly salted water over high heat. Once boiling, lower the heat to low and carefully place the eggs into the pot to cook for 6 minutes. Remove and place into an ice bath to cool down, 2 to 3 minutes. Alternatively, run the eggs under cold water until they have cooled down.

Make the marinade: In medium-sized pot over medium heat, combine all the marinade ingredients with 3 cups (710 ml) of water. Simmer for about 10 minutes, then remove from the heat and let cool down. Discard the teabags.

To prepare the eggs, carefully crack each shell all over with the back of a spoon. If the shell is not cracked enough, the marinade will have less chance to color and flavor the eggs. Once cracked, place the eggs into a small, lidded container and pour in the marinade liquid. Leave the eggs to marinate for at least 24 hours, refrigerated.

When ready to eat, peel and enjoy cold or at room temperature.

SPRING ONION FLOWER ROLLS

Here, we are taking a basic *bao* bun dough and adding a simple spring onion–based oil. Instead of your standard proof-proof-steam situation (which can take a little extra time), you can speed things up by making your dough and just doing a single 10-minute proof.

These rolls are a potsticker situation—brown them on the bottom first, add some water into the pan, put the lid on and steam away! The flower-shaped twist is a unique dough technique, but one that's easy and impressive. As with pancakes, you can expect to have to dip them in something saucy—or just scarf down three or four on their own.

MAKES 1 DOZEN ROLLS

Bao Dough

⅓ cup + 2 tsp (100 ml) milk, at room temperature

⅓ cup + 2 tsp (100 ml) water, at room temperature

2 tbsp (26 g) superfine sugar

1 (0.25-oz) package (7 g) instant yeast

10.5 oz (300 g) steamed bun flour (see note), plus more for dusting

Pinch of salt

¼ cup (60 ml) vegetable oil

½ cup (50 g) finely chopped spring onion

½ tsp Chinese five-spice powder

Salt

NOTE:

- Steamed bun flour can be found at most Asian grocery stores.

Make the dough: In a large liquid measuring cup, combine the milk, water, superfine sugar and yeast. Stir well and set aside for 5 minutes for the yeast to activate. In the bowl of a stand mixer fitted with the dough hook attachment, combine the bun flour and yeast mixture while mixing on low speed. Work up to medium speed, then add salt. Mix on medium speed for 10 minutes, or until smooth.

Remove the mixing bowl from your mixer, cover with plastic wrap and set aside to proof for about 30 minutes. Remove the dough from the bowl, reknead briefly and roll into a thin rectangle about 8 x 12 inches (20 x 30 cm) in size, dusting with extra flour, if required.

Brush the sheet of dough lightly with vegetable oil and sprinkle evenly with spring onion, Chinese five-spice powder and salt. Fold the dough twice from the long side to make a strip that has three layers, then cut into 12 pieces.

To form a flower roll, work with two pieces at a time, stacking them on top of each other in a vertical line. Place a chopstick horizontally at the halfway point and press down. Flip so the dough hangs from the chopstick and while holding both ends of the dough, stretch while twisting the chopstick. Place the twisted roll back on your counter, press the chopstick down and slide it out of the roll. Continue until the remaining flower rolls are formed. Place each roll onto a piece of parchment paper and let rest for another 30 minutes, until slightly risen.

Working in batches, place the rolls 1 inch (2.5 cm) apart in a steamer basket. Pour enough water into a wok until the water line is 1 inch (2.5 cm) below the bottom of the steamer. Once the water is boiling, cover and steam your flower rolls for 8 to 10 minutes, or until cooked through. As an extra step, you can panfry these in a nonstick skillet with a little oil, if desired. Serve immediately.

VEGAN FRIED KOREAN "CHICKEN"

Plant-based alternatives to meat are on the rise, but in reality, wheat meat is a substitute that's been around for more than 1,000 years. Seitan (vital wheat gluten) is made from flour by essentially removing all the starches, leaving behind a "dough" that is about three times higher in protein than red meat.

SERVES 2 TO 4

Vegan "Chicken"

1 (14-oz [400-g]) can chickpeas, undrained

2 tbsp + 1 tsp (35 ml) water

1 tbsp (6 g) vegetable stock powder

1 tbsp (15 ml) white wine vinegar

2 tsp (5 g) onion powder

1 tsp garlic powder

Scant 2 oz (50 g) silken tofu

7 oz (200 g) vital wheat gluten

Coating Mixture

4 tbsp (30 g) chickpea flour

¾ cup + 2 tsp (200 ml) unsweetened soy milk

1 tsp rice vinegar

½ tsp gochujang (Korean chili paste)

Flour Mixture

10.5 oz (300 g) all-purpose flour

3 tbsp (24 g) cornstarch

2 tsp (12 g) salt

Vegetable oil, for frying

Sweet-and-Sour Sauce

4 tbsp (60 ml) honey

4 tbsp (60 ml) soy sauce

3 cloves garlic, finely grated

½ tsp finely grated fresh ginger

3 tbsp (45 ml) rice vinegar

2 tbsp (30 ml) hoisin sauce

1 tbsp (15 ml) toasted sesame oil

Make the "chicken": In a high-speed food processor or blender, combine the chickpeas (and the liquid from the can), water, vegetable stock powder, white wine vinegar, onion powder, garlic powder and silken tofu. Blend on high speed until smooth, then transfer to a large bowl. Add the wheat gluten and stir until you get a spongy dough. Tip out onto your counter and knead until it becomes smooth and stretchy. Pinch off ¾-inch (2-cm) chunks of dough and place in a steamer basket lined with parchment paper. Cover and steam over low heat for 50 minutes, topping up the water in the bottom of the pan as needed. Remove from the heat, let cool and set aside.

Fry the "chicken": In a medium-sized bowl, combine the coating mixture ingredients and whisk well. In a separate bowl, combine all the flour mixture ingredients and stir well. Dunk a piece of "chicken" in the coating mixture, then into the flour mixture. Do this again carefully and place on a tray.

Fill a wok about two-thirds full with vegetable oil. Heat over medium-high heat to 350°F (180°C) and test by dipping a wooden chopstick into the oil: The chopstick will sizzle when the oil is ready. Working in batches, gently lower the "chicken" into the oil and cook until golden brown, 3 to 5 minutes. Drain on a plate lined with paper towels and keep warm while you make the sauce.

Make the sweet-and-sour sauce: In a small pot over medium heat, combine all the sauce ingredients and bring to a boil. Cook, stirring, for a few minutes, until the sauce thickens and becomes sticky. If it becomes too sticky, add a little water to thin it out. Transfer the "chicken" to a serving platter. While the sauce is hot, drizzle it over the "chicken" and serve immediately.

MUM'S CRISPY PORK WONTONS

Grandmère does her wontons with prawns the classic way, but at most of our family dinners, our go-to meat is pork. That's what my mum likes to put in her wontons, and I'm excited to share her variation on Grandmère's recipe with you.

As wontons are small anyway, a little ground pork can make a lot of wontons without breaking the bank. For those of us who don't eat pork, ground chicken will make a fine substitute, too, but don't compromise on the fattiness—that's what keeps the wontons juicy.

MAKES 30 WONTONS

Filling

10.5 oz (300 g) fatty ground pork

4 tbsp (60 ml) oyster sauce

1 tsp sesame oil

1 tsp finely grated fresh ginger

1 tsp cornstarch

Pinch of freshly ground white pepper

Pinch of salt

30 wonton wrappers

Spicy Mayo

1 cup (225 g) Kewpie brand mayonnaise

3 tbsp (45 ml) sriracha

Vegetable oil, for wok

Make the filling: In a bowl, combine all the filling ingredients and mix vigorously in one direction until the mixture binds. Cover and leave to rest in the fridge for 30 minutes.

Working with one dumpling wrapper at a time, place 1 heaping teaspoon of filling in the center of a wrapper. Brush half of the edges of the square with water. Fold the wet edges over (in half) to make a triangle shape and enclose the filling. Brush one of the corners with water and fold inward to overlap with the other corner. Press to seal. Cover loosely with a clean, damp tea towel and repeat the process to form the remaining wontons.

Make the spicy mayo: In a small bowl, mix together the mayonnaise and sriracha until well combined. Set aside.

When ready to cook the wontons, fill a wok about two-thirds full with vegetable oil. Heat over medium-high heat to 350°F (180°C) and test by dipping a wooden chopstick into the oil: The chopstick will sizzle when the oil is ready. Working in batches, gently lower the wontons into the oil and cook until golden brown, 3 to 5 minutes. Drain on a plate lined with paper towels and serve immediately with the spicy mayo.

XINJIANG LAMB SKEWERS

You might have seen me make this recipe on *MasterChef*, served with biang biang noodles. In a different form, but still one of my personal favorites, is Xinjiang lamb.

Northwestern China showcases flavors so characteristic of Middle Eastern and Chinese fusion, representing one of the many diverse cultural identities in which China is rich. The classic way to have Xinjiang lamb is marinated, loaded with spices and nicely charred on a barbecue grill. No hibachi grill needed, but it's important to make sure the grill is smoking hot.

SERVES 4

2¼ lb (1 kg) lamb shoulder

Marinade

¼ cup (60 ml) vegetable oil

2 tbsp (30 ml) light soy sauce

2 tsp (5 g) cornstarch

1 tsp salt

½ tsp superfine sugar

1 tsp ground fennel seeds

2 tsp ground cilantro seeds

1 tbsp (7 g) ground cumin

½ tsp chili powder

¼ tsp freshly ground Sichuan peppercorns (optional)

To Serve

Ground cumin

Chili powder (optional)

Fresh lime juice

To prepare the lamb, debone and cut it into 1-inch (2.5-cm) cubes. Place the lamb cubes into a bowl along with all ingredients for the marinade and mix until well combined. Cover and refrigerate to marinate for a minimum of 2 hours (ideally overnight).

Soak eight bamboo skewers for 30 minutes. Then, working with one skewer at a time, thread the lamb cubes closely onto them. Continue until all the lamb has been threaded. Grill the skewers on high heat, turning frequently, until the lamb becomes browned and lightly charred on all surfaces, about 10 to 15 minutes. Sprinkle with additional ground cumin and chili powder, if desired, during this process. Serve immediately with a small squeeze of fresh lime.

MOUTHWATERING SICHUAN CHICKEN

The Chinese name for this dish translates to "saliva chicken" in English. Rest assured, no actual saliva is required. The name reflects the mouthwatering effect it has while it is being eaten (and definitely while anticipating the eating). Chinese black vinegar, chili oil and Sichuan peppercorns make for a tangy, spicy, numbing sauce that will leave you salivating.

The focus point is the succulent chicken. This is achieved through boiling briefly with some subtle aromatics, then letting the chicken gently cook as the heat is gradually lowered, with a final blanching in ice water. This keeps the chicken moist and gives a firm outer texture at the same time. I'm salivating right now.

SERVES 4

1¾ lb (800 g) chicken thighs, skin on

4 slices fresh ginger

2 spring onions, white part only

1 tbsp (15 ml) Shaoxing rice wine

Sichuan Sauce

6 tbsp (90 ml) Chinese Chili Oil (page 147)

2 tbsp (30 ml) Chinese black vinegar

1 tbsp (15 ml) light soy sauce

1 tbsp (15 ml) sesame oil

2 tbsp (30 ml) Shaoxing rice wine

1½ tsp (6 g) superfine sugar

2 cloves garlic, finely minced

1 spring onion, white part only, finely minced

1 tbsp (1 g) minced fresh cilantro

To Serve

Chopped roasted peanuts,

Toasted white sesame seeds

Fresh cilantro leaves

Cook the chicken: In a large pot, combine the thigh pieces along with the ginger, spring onion white parts and Shaoxing wine. Fill with water until the chicken is just covered. Bring to a boil over high heat, then lower the heat and let simmer for 10 minutes. Turn off heat and let sit with the lid on for another 10 minutes.

Fill a large bowl with ice water and transfer the chicken to the bowl to stop the cooking process. Remove the chicken, pat dry and slice into ¾-inch (2-cm)-thick slices. Transfer to a serving bowl.

Make the sauce: In a small bowl, combine all the dressing ingredients and stir well until the sugar has dissolved. Pour the sauce over the chicken and top with roasted peanuts and sesame seeds. Garnish with cilantro leaves.

JAPANESE BRAISED PORK BELLY (CHASHU)

What noodle book would be complete without a *chashu* recipe? Ramen is arguably one of the most revered types of noodle soups, and any ramen lovers would recognize chashu as the delicious braised pork that must go on top.

Although I've kept to a more traditional Japanese-style chashu, braised pork is fairly versatile and will complement many of the other noodle dishes in this book. While the sear is not super traditional for chashu, I like to caramelize the meat first to bring out the sugars and fats before anything else is added, to make sure the pork's flavor is as good as it can be throughout the braising.

SERVES 8 TO 10

2¼ lb (1 kg) pork belly, skin removed (about 8 x 13" [20 x 23 cm])

1 tbsp (15 ml) vegetable oil

2 spring onions, white part only

1 slice fresh ginger

5 dried shiitake mushrooms

½ cup (120 ml) sake

½ cup (120 ml) mirin

1 cup (240 ml) soy sauce

⅔ cup (133 g) sugar

Roll the pork belly tightly into a cylindrical shape and tie up, wrapping it with kitchen twine so it holds. In a large skillet over high heat, heat the vegetable oil. Add the rolled pork belly and sear on all surfaces, turning, for about 15 minutes.

Transfer the seared pork to a large pot and add all the remaining ingredients, plus enough water to cover (at least 2 cups [475 ml]). Bring to a boil, then lower the heat to low and simmer for 2 hours, rotating the pork every 30 minutes.

Once the meat has cooled, transfer to a container and refrigerate overnight. Remove the twine and slice into scant ¼-inch (6-mm)-thick slices. Place the slices on a plate and sear quickly with a kitchen torch. Serve as desired.

NINE

NOODLE CONDIMENT ESSENTIALS

I can handle a basic meal, but it's gotta have all the sauces. Every dish that goes out at Bumplings has a minimum of two condiments because I am all about the condiment life. Even if there is nothing meal worthy in the fridge or pantry, the one thing that I always have in excess is sauces, dressings and condiments. Whether it's a feast or two-minute noodles—whatever meal you put together gets an instant upgrade from adding condiments. Here's a few recipes so you can have condiments on hand, too—some from the Bumplings kitchen and some from my own at home.

GINGER AND SPRING ONION OIL

I am a devout fan of Hainanese chicken rice. I'm split on whether it's the succulent chicken I love the most or if it's the oil that goes on top, as it goes well with just about anything. This rendition is a bit of a hack. No infusion required, just the you po–style hot oil poured over aromatics, herbs and spices.

MAKES ABOUT ¾ CUP (200 ML)

---

1 cup + 2 tbsp (60 g) finely minced spring onion, white part only

½ cup (40 g) finely minced fresh ginger

½ cup + 1 tsp (125 ml) vegetable oil

4 tsp (20 ml) toasted sesame oil

2 tsp (12 g) salt

In a small, heatproof bowl, combine the spring onion and ginger. In a wok over high heat, heat the vegetable oil. Once the oil hits 350°F (180°C), it will start shimmering. Carefully pour the hot oil over the spring onion and ginger. Add the toasted sesame oil and salt, and mix well. Serve as required.

CHINESE CHILI OIL

This is a bit of a modification of my original Sichuan-style chili oil, and I always have a jar of this on standby in the pantry. It carries many of the same spices and flavors, but I've toned them down and added some other elements for more widespread use and versatility, so you're not locked into cooking Sichuan food all the time.

MAKES ABOUT 1 CUP (240 ML)

---

1 cup + 2 tsp (250 ml) vegetable oil

1 cinnamon stick

3 star anise

1 tbsp (6 g) fennel seeds

2 tbsp (10 g) Sichuan peppercorns

2 bay leaves

6 green cardamom pods

¼ cup (25 g) crushed red pepper flakes

2 tbsp (7 g) Korean chili flakes

Pinch of salt

In a small saucepan over low heat, combine the vegetable oil, cinnamon stick, star anise, fennel seeds, Sichuan peppercorns, bay leaves and cardamom pods, and cook until the oil becomes fragrant, about 25 minutes. It is very easy to burn your spices at this point, so check in every now and then and adjust the heat as required. Meanwhile, in a medium-sized heatproof bowl, combine the crushed red pepper flakes, Korean chili flakes and salt. Once the oil is fragrant, increase the heat to high and cook for another 30 seconds. Carefully strain the oil through a fine sieve into the bowl that contains the chili flake mixture, and stir well. It should sizzle and change color immediately. Let cool to room temperature before using.

THE OG CHILI SAUCE

Sriracha is the perfect addition for any recipes that need a bit of livening up. Ones that are already a bit heavy in the oil department (such as Mum's Crispy Pork Wontons [page 136]) won't need too much additional benefit from any chili oil, but could definitely use a tangy acidic hit of red chile to cut through the oil. I like mine on smashed avo and eggs, too.

MAKES ABOUT 1¼ CUPS (300 ML)

12.5 oz (350 g) long red chiles

6 cloves garlic

⅓ cup (120 ml) distilled white vinegar

1 tbsp (15 ml) water

1 tbsp (18 g) salt

1 tbsp (15 g) raw sugar

Juice of 1 lime

Prepare your chiles by slicing in half lengthwise and removing all the seeds and pith (see note). Place the chiles, garlic, vinegar and water in a blender and blend until smooth. Transfer your mixture to a small pot over medium heat and add the salt and raw sugar. Bring to a boil, then lower the heat to low and cook, stirring constantly, until reduced to a thicker consistency. Stirring the mixture is important to prevent the bottom from burning. Once you are happy with the consistency, remove from the heat and stir in the lime juice. Taste and season as desired.

NOTE:

- Make sure to wear gloves when handling chiles.

PEANUT SAUCE

In a book full of spicy stuff, it's good to have something in here that's quenching, cooling and creamy. I think this one speaks for itself.

MAKES ABOUT 1¼ CUPS (300 ML)

½ cup (120 ml) coconut milk

½ cup (128 g) smooth peanut butter

1 tbsp (15 g) red curry paste

1 tbsp (15 ml) sweet soy sauce

1 tbsp (15 ml) soy sauce

2 tbsp (30 ml) pure maple syrup

½ cup (120 ml) water

½ tsp salt

In a small saucepan over medium heat, combine all the ingredients and whisk until smooth. Lower the heat to low and simmer, stirring, until thickened. Taste and season as desired.

TEN

NOODLE DOUGH & SHAPES

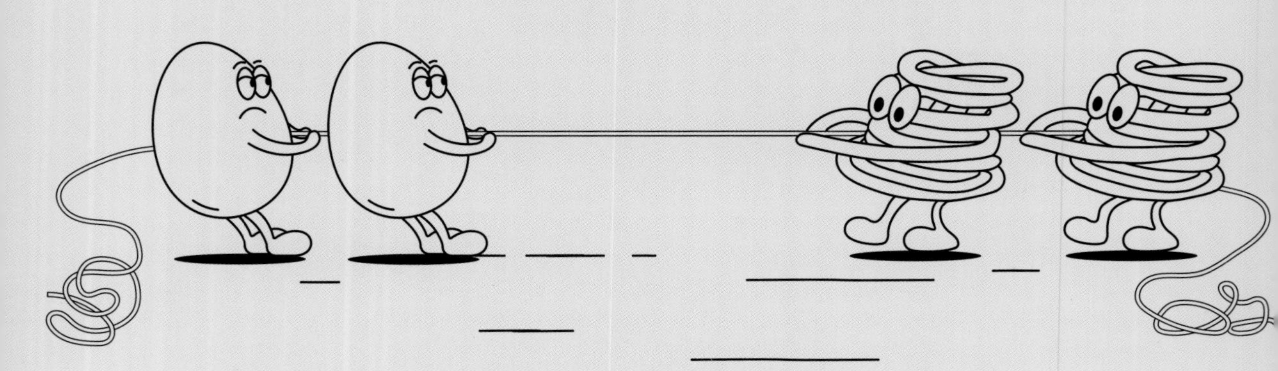

HAND-CUT WHEAT NOODLES

These are probably my favorite noodles to make from scratch, and they're especially great for first-timers! All you need are two ingredients (flour and water), clean hands and a knife. No fancy machine is necessary either. And all you have to do to create these wonderful noodles is simply to slice the dough with the knife. What's also great about making these noodles is they don't all have to be the same shape or thickness, so you can slice up a bowl of noodles pretty quickly and the varying texture and shapes are part of the taste experience too! That said, make sure you don't slice them too thickly, though!

MAKES ABOUT 1 POUND (450 G)

10.5 oz (300 g) bread flour
¼ tsp salt
5 oz (150 ml) water
Cornstarch, for dusting

In the bowl of a stand mixer fitted with the dough hook attachment, combine the bread flour and salt. Start on low speed and gradually add the water, allowing for the flour to absorb each addition. You can do this by hand, too! A rough textured dough will form after 3 minutes of kneading. Increase the speed slightly and continue to knead for 10 minutes, or until smooth. If you are kneading by hand, knead for 15 minutes.

Remove the bowl, cover with plastic wrap and allow to rest for 30 minutes. The dough will continue to absorb moisture and become more pliable. Knead for another 2 minutes, then cut in half to form two portions.

Lightly dust your counter with cornstarch and roll one portion into a long rectangular sheet. Follow the steps below for different wheat noodle shapes.

For thin noodles: Roll out as thinly as you can with a rolling pin, 1/32 to 1/16 inch (1 to 2 mm) thick. Dust each side of the sheet, then fold into four layers. Cut strips 1/32 to 1/16 inch (1 to 2 mm) wide, using a dry sharp knife. Dust with additional cornstarch and gently separate the noodle strips to prevent sticking.

For thicker udon-style noodles: Roll out to ⅛ inch (3 mm) thick with a rolling pin. Dust each side of the sheet, then fold into four layers. Cut strips ⅛ inch (3 mm) wide, using a dry sharp knife. Dust with additional cornstarch and gently separate the noodle strips to avoid sticking.

For flat ribbon-style noodles: Roll out to 1/32 to 1/16 inch (1 to 2 mm) thick with a rolling pin. Dust each side of the sheet, then fold into four layers. Cut strips 1¼ inch (3 cm) wide, using a dry sharp knife. Dust with additional cornstarch and gently separate the noodle strips to prevent sticking.

Cook in a large pot of boiling water for 2 to 3 minutes, or until just cooked through. If you are not cooking the noodles immediately, toss with some cornstarch and refrigerate, separated into batches, in airtight bags.

NOTE:

- Bread flour is also known as strong flour or high-gluten flour. If the mixer fails to bring the dough together, turn off the mixer and push the dough together with your hands.

HAND-SMACKED NOODLES

Also known as biang biang noodles, these are hand-smacked into shape by taking your dough and slapping it up and down on your kitchen counter. *Biang* refers to the shape of these noodles, being thick, flat and wide like a belt, but I think it also relates to the sound it makes as it stretches and slaps on the counter. A really fun noodle to make and you get a bit of a cardio work out, too, so it's a win-win!

MAKES ABOUT 1 POUND (455 G)

10.5 oz (300 g) all-purpose flour, plus more for dusting

Pinch of salt

½ cup + 7 tsp (155 ml) water, plus more as needed

Vegetable oil, for coating

In the bowl of a stand mixer fitted with a dough hook attachment, combine the flour and salt. Start on low speed and slowly add the water. If the dough is a little dry, add an additional tablespoon (15 ml) of water at a time. Increase the speed to medium and let knead for 10 to 15 minutes, or until smooth and elastic. Cover with plastic wrap and let rest for 1 hour.

Line a baking sheet with parchment paper and set aside. Brush a clean work surface with vegetable oil and press the dough into a rectangle that is about ½ inch (1.3 cm) in thickness. Cut into 10 equal strips, laying them flat on the counter. Pick up one noodle, holding it on both ends, slapping it repeatedly onto the work surface while stretching it to about 8-inch (20-cm)-long ribbons. Place your noodles on the prepared baking sheet and repeat the process. Cover with plastic wrap to prevent drying out, then set aside until required.

Bring a large pot of water to a boil. Cook the noodles for 2 to 3 minutes, or until just cooked through. These noodles must be made fresh and cooked. They do not keep well refrigerated.

EGG NOODLES

As the name suggests, this noodle is primarily made of flour and egg, and is the base noodle for countless favorites around the world. The addition of the egg to the dough provides so much more than flavor—the noodle dough is resilient, silky in texture and richer in flavor—allowing it to be much more versatile than many other noodles, hence it offers an excellent foundation for creativity!

MAKES ABOUT 28 OUNCES (800 G)

17.5 oz (500 g) all-purpose flour
1 tsp salt
6 large eggs
Cornstarch, for dusting

In the bowl of a stand mixer fitted with a dough hook attachment, combine the flour and salt. Start on low speed and gradually add the eggs, allowing for the flour to absorb each addition. You can do this by hand, too!

A rough-textured dough will form after 3 minutes of kneading. Increase the speed slightly and continue to knead for 10 minutes, or until smooth. If you are kneading by hand, knead for 15 minutes. Wrap the dough in plastic wrap and let rest at room temperature for 30 minutes.

Once the dough has rested, remove it from the plastic wrap, and knead for 3 minutes. Divide the dough into two equal portions, wrap in fresh plastic wrap and let rest for an additional 30 minutes at room temperature.

After the dough has rested for the second time, dust your counter with cornstarch and, working with one portion at a time, follow the steps below for different egg noodle shapes.

For thin noodles: Roll out as thinly as you can with a rolling pin, 1/32 to 1/16 inch (1 to 2 mm) thick. Dust each side of the sheet, then fold into four layers. Cut strips 1/32 to 1/16 inch (1 to 2 mm), using a dry sharp knife. Dust with additional cornstarch and gently separate the noodle strips to prevent sticking.

For thick noodles: Roll out to 1/8 inch (3 mm) thick with a rolling pin. Dust each side of the sheet, then fold into four layers. Cut strips 1/8 inch (3 mm) wide, using a dry sharp knife. Dust with additional cornstarch and gently separate the noodle strips to prevent sticking.

Cook in a large pot of boiling water for 2 to 3 minutes, or until just cooked through. If you are not cooking the noodles immediately, toss with some cornstarch and refrigerate, separated into batches, in airtight bags.

RICE NOODLE SHEETS

These noodle sheets are best eaten fresh, so it really is worth making them from scratch! I absolutely love their slippery silky texture, and they're also excellent "carriers" of flavor. These can be found in some noodle soup or gravy dishes, and also are commonly used to wrap or roll with different fillings inside.

MAKES 15 RICE NOODLE SHEETS

---

2 tsp (10 g) mung bean starch
5.5 oz (150 g) rice starch
7½ tbsp (60 g) tapioca starch
1¾ cups + 7 tsp (450 ml) water
Vegetable oil spray, for pan

In a large bowl, roughly combine the mung bean starch, rice starch and tapioca starch, and slowly whisk in the water. Continue to whisk the batter until well mixed, then cover and leave to sit at room temperature for 30 minutes. After 30 minutes, the batter should be well hydrated.

Bring a large pot of water fitted with a steamer basket to a boil. The water level should be below the basket. Once boiling, lower the heat to medium.

Oil a 6-inch (15-cm) round cake pan with vegetable oil or spray. A small pizza pan or heatproof dish will work fine instead, as long as it fits inside the steamer. This will be used to make the flat steamed rice noodle sheets.

Transfer the rice noodle batter into a large liquid measuring cup and ensure it is mixed well before pouring. Pour in just enough batter to coat the bottom of the prepared cake pan, then place the pan in the steamer and put the lid on the steamer. Steam for 2 to 3 minutes, or until the sheet has solidified. Remove from the steamer and allow to cool slightly; then gently coat the sheet with thin layer of vegetable oil spray.

Once the cake pan is just cool enough to touch, carefully peel off the steamed rice noodle sheet, using a palette knife or silicone spatula and transfer to a large plate.

Oil the cake pan again and repeat the procedure until all the rice noodle batter is used.

Arrange all the steamed rice noodle sheets into a stack and use as the recipe requires. If making wide noodles, cut them into your desired width, using a dry sharp knife. Transfer all the rice noodles to a bowl, coat with more oil as required to prevent them sticking, cover and set aside.

If you are not using the rice noodles/sheets immediately, refrigerate the cooked noodles, well coated with vegetable oil, in airtight containers. Fresh rice noodles will keep for up to 2 days like this.

THIN RICE NOODLES

It's actually quite easy to tell the difference between store-bought rice noodles and freshly made rice noodles. The latter are far more superior, with greater buoyancy and silkiness—they're actually not that hard to make at home! There are so many different applications, and most I can't get enough of, but I find these rice noodles are best when stir-fried or added to soup.

MAKES ABOUT 1½ POUNDS (670 G)

---

2 tsp (10 g) mung bean starch
5.5 oz (150 g) rice starch
2 oz + 1 tsp (60 g) tapioca starch
1¾ cups + 7 tsp (450 ml) water

NOTES:

- A piping bag is an easy substitute for the potato ricer if you don't have one at home. Just put the smallest nozzle on the piping bag and simply squeeze streams of the paste into the water.
- To make thick rice noodles, cut the tip of the piping bag to about ⅛ inch (3 mm) in diameter to allow for a thicker noodle.

In a large bowl, roughly combine the mung bean starch, rice starch and tapioca starch, and slowly whisk in the water. Continue to whisk the batter until well mixed, cover and leave to sit at room temperature for 30 minutes. After 30 minutes, the batter should be well hydrated. In a microwave-safe bowl, microwave the batter for 1 to 2 minutes on high, removing the bowl and stirring intermittently, until the batter forms a thick paste.

Bring a large pot of water to a boil and lower the heat to medium once boiling. Using a potato ricer with the finest setting (see notes), load a ladle of rice noodle paste into the chamber and gently extrude into the pot of boiling water. Cook the thin rice noodles for 2 to 3 minutes, or until they begin to float to the water's surface.

Using tongs or a pasta scoop, gently remove cooked rice noodles from the boiling water and place into a large bowl of cold or ice water. Drain, once cool, using a colander.

Reload the potato ricer with another scoop of the rice noodle paste and repeat the procedure until all the paste is used.

Put all cooked rice noodles into a bowl and gently rinse before use.

If you are not using the noodles immediately, refrigerate the cooked noodles, well coated with vegetable oil, in airtight containers. Fresh rice noodles will keep for up to 2 days like this.

SWEET POTATO NOODLES

These are a type of transparent noodle made from, you guessed it, sweet potato flour. They are commonly mistaken for rice noodles but have a stronger, bouncier quality that allows them to maintain their beautiful texture in a variety of dishes. I also like to use them as a filler for things like spring rolls and dumplings.

MAKES ABOUT 15 OUNCES (420 G)

6 oz (170 g) sweet potato starch

Pinch of salt

½ cup + 1 tsp (125 ml) boiling water

½ cup + 1 tsp (125 ml) water, at room temperature

In a large, heatproof bowl, combine the sweet potato starch and pinch of salt. Using chopsticks or a whisk, slowly add the *boiling* water, mixing constantly, until a rough dough is formed. Once cool, carefully knead for 5 minutes, or until a smooth dough comes together.

Add the room-temperature water to the bowl and mix into the dough until it becomes a thick, opaque batter. Let rest, covered, at room temperature for 30 minutes to properly hydrate the starch.

Bring a large pot of water to a boil and lower the heat to medium once boiling. After the dough has rested, load the thickened batter into a piping bag with a small circular nozzle (see note), then gently squeeze a continuous ribbon of the batter into the pot of boiling water until a thin layer covers the bottom of the pot. Cook the noodles for 2 to 3 minutes, stirring occasionally, until they begin to float to the water's surface. They should take on a translucent appearance once cooked.

Using tongs or a pasta scoop, gently remove the cooked noodles from the pot and place into a large bowl of cold or ice water, then drain, using a colander, once cool. Working in batches, continue to squeeze out ribbons of the starch batter into the boiling water, until all batter is used up.

Put all the cooked sweet potato noodles into a bowl and gently rinse before use.

If you are not using the noodles immediately, refrigerate the cooked noodles, well coated with vegetable oil, in an airtight container. Fresh sweet potato noodles will keep for up to 2 days like this.

NOTE:

- Sweet potato starch is sometimes difficult to find, so it can easily be replaced with standard potato starch or pea starch. For wide sweet potato noodles, use the wide rectangular ribbon nozzle with the piping bag instead of the small circular nozzle.

MUNG BEAN (JELLY) NOODLES

The jelly noodles, made from mung bean starch, turn bright white upon cooking and have a slightly bouncy texture—like jelly! Unlike most noodles, these noodles are made from hot water and, traditionally, served best when cold. If you've not tried these noodles, I'd highly recommend giving them a taste—you won't regret it.

MAKES SLIGHTLY LESS THAN 1½ POUNDS (665 G)

2⅓ cups (580 ml) water
3 oz (85 g) mung bean starch
Vegetable oil or spray, for coating

NOTE:

- Heating the mung bean jelly very briefly in a microwave, about 10 seconds, can help loosen it if you have difficulty coercing it out of the container; however, be sure your container is microwave-safe before doing this.

In a large bowl, combine half of the water (290 ml) with the mung bean starch and mix until the starch is dissolved and a thin white batter is formed.

In a medium-sized saucepan, bring the remaining water to a boil. Once boiling, quickly add the batter while stirring vigorously until fully combined with the boiling water. Lower the heat to medium and continue to cook while stirring constantly. Cook for around 5 minutes, or until the batter turns translucent and becomes very thick in consistency.

Turn off the heat and continue to slowly stir the thickened mung bean paste for around 5 minutes, allowing it to cool down slightly. Oil a deep 8 x 12–inch (20 x 30–cm) glass baking dish or heatproof container with the vegetable oil or spray, then carefully pour in the thickened mung bean paste, leveling out where possible, for consistency.

Let cool, uncovered, at room temperature for about 1 hour, before covering and refrigerate overnight or until the mung bean paste sets like jelly, about 3 hours.

Once set, invert the mung bean jelly (see note) onto a clean chopping board in preparation for forming the mung bean jelly noodles.

For thicker noodles (such as the liang fen): Cut ¼-inch (6-mm)-wide slices along the width of the mung bean jelly rectangle, using a dry sharp knife. Stack these slices, then cut again to a ¼-inch (6-mm) thickness, or as desired.

For thinner noodles: Use a Microplane, hand grater or peeler and firmly run it along the length of the mung bean jelly rectangle.

Once your noodles are formed, collect into a bowl, coat and toss with a little vegetable oil, then set aside.

If you are not using the noodles immediately, refrigerate the cooked noodles, well coated with vegetable oil, in an airtight container. Freshly made mung bean noodles will keep for up to 2 days like this.

BUCKWHEAT (SOBA) NOODLES

A favorite in many Asian cultures, these are another one of the easier noodles to make, and always a crowd pleaser when fresh. Soba noodles are tender yet chewy thin noodles made from buckwheat flour. In Japan, they are traditionally served cold with dipping sauce or in soup, but I also love using them in salads!

MAKES ABOUT 13.5 OUNCES (380 G)

---

6 oz (170 g) buckwheat flour

1.5 oz (45 g) tapioca starch, plus more for dusting

Scant tsp (5 g) salt, plus 1 tbsp (18 g) for cooking

⅔ cup + 1 tsp (165 ml) boiling water, plus more as needed

Vegetable oil, if using

In the bowl of a stand mixer fitted with a dough hook attachment, combine the buckwheat flour, tapioca starch and salt. Start on low speed and slowly incorporate the boiling water until all is added. Increase the speed to medium and let knead for 10 to 15 minutes, or until smooth. As there is no gluten in buckwheat flour, the dough will not be elastic and soft like wheat-based doughs.

If the dough is still a little dry after kneading, add 1 additional tablespoon (15 ml) of water at a time and knead for another minute or two. The dough should be smooth, but very dense and hard. Cover with plastic wrap and rest for 1 hour.

After the dough rests, lightly dust your counter with extra tapioca starch. Cut your dough into two portions, setting one aside under a clean, moist tea towel (see note) until ready to use, and roll out the other portion into a long rectangular sheet.

For traditional soba noodles: Roll out as thinly as you can with a rolling pin, about 1⁄32 to 1⁄16 inch (1 to 2 mm) wide. Dust each side of the dough sheet well with tapioca starch, then fold into four layers. Cut strips 1⁄32 to 1⁄16 inch (1 to 2 mm) wide, using a dry sharp knife.

Once your noodles are cut, collect into a large bowl and dust them well with additional tapioca starch, ensuring the noodles don't stick together.

Bring a large pot of water to a boil with an extra tablespoon (18 g) of salt and lower the heat to medium once boiling. Place handfuls of the soba noodles into the pot and cook for 4 to 5 minutes, or until the texture softens. Once cooked, remove the noodles, using tongs or a pasta scoop, and rinse under cool water in a colander. Once cooled, set aside the cooked noodles in a bowl and toss with vegetable oil to prevent them sticking together. Working in batches, continue to cook the noodles until all the dough is used.

If you are not using the noodles immediately, refrigerate the cooked noodles, well coated with oil, in an airtight container. Freshly made buckwheat noodles will keep for up to 2 days like this.

NOTE:

- If buckwheat flour isn't available, whole wheat or spelt flour makes a great substitute. Buckwheat soba noodles are renowned for drying out and cracking, so make sure to keep a clean, moist tea towel handy to prevent this from happening.

ACKNOWLEDGMENTS

First, thank you to all my extended family members and staff at Bumplings who have helped me with this book. There are so many ways you all inspire me, from new recipe ideas on the menu to trying out trendy restaurants. Every food moment together has helped shape me as a cook and as a writer.

Mum (Dany)—There would be no cookbook without you. I am grateful for all the love and encouragement you give me each day. Writing this book was indeed one of my biggest challenges, and you were there every step of the way.

Grandmère (Josephine) and Grandpère (Clement)—Thank you for being so excited about cooking and sharing your knowledge with me. You have been my biggest inspiration in the kitchen!

To my younger brothers (Brad, Liam and Josh), thanks for always supporting me, no matter what! It's been a tough year, but you guys have been there. This book is a testament of your support.

Dad (Richard)—Some of my most memorable and loving food experiences have been with you, both in the kitchen and out. It brings me so much joy knowing that food is one of the big things in life that brings us together. Thank you for always pushing me to do my best and for pushing me to document my recipes.

Melvin—I can't thank you enough for your generosity and support in writing this book. It's a shame the chocolate noodles didn't make the cut, but I am excited to share many weird and wonderful food experiences together in the future.

ABOUT THE AUTHOR

Brendan Pang is a Western Australian cook who specializes in working with dough in both modern adaptations and traditional styles of Chinese cuisine to create dumplings, buns and noodles.

Born in the capital city of Perth, Brendan has lived a life rich in cultural experiences, being welcomed into the culture of the Yawuru people in Western Australia's northwest, and from his upbringing in a Chinese Mauritian family.

Dumplings and wontons have been a major part of Brendan's life, and so too have noodles. Although Chinese Mauritian culture has developed its own cultural identity for quite some time, some Chinese traditions are still conserved and maintained in Chinese Mauritian families like Brendan's. Every Chinese New Year in Brendan's family features foong pow, the *yee sang* prosperity salad and long-life noodles freshly made by Grandmère Josephine. Many members of Brendan's family work with doughs and batters in their businesses and crafts—his mother, Dany, making cakes; his brother Brad making donuts; and his aunty Cathy making pizza. So many fond memories are associated with dough, batters and noodles for Brendan and his family, and so they will continue to be for many years to come.

After starring on *MasterChef Australia* season 10, Brendan spent much of his time launching his food concept: Bumplings, where he began to explore the use of dough in dumplings and other Chinese Mauritian foods. Nearly 12 months after starting Bumplings, Brendan released his very first cookbook, *This Is a Book About Dumplings*. At the same time, he starred again on *MasterChef Australia* season 12 "Back to Win," and his passion for working with dough and ability to express his creativity using it was expanded from dumplings to buns and noodles. His passions were fortunately not greatly impacted by the COVID-19 crisis in Western Australia, so he was able to continue to explore this passion with his head chef, Meg, leading him to write his second cookbook.

After launching a frozen dumpling range in 2020, Brendan and Meg have developed Bumplings further, to make a regularly changing menu with new dishes as well as an expanding catering branch of Bumplings. Much of his focus in 2021 has also been directed toward the launch of his own cooking school. Brendan takes great pride in his cooking school and in teaching other people how to make dumplings, buns, noodles and more.

INDEX